A
Brighter
Word
Than
Bright

MUSE
BOOKS
THE IOWA SERIES
IN CREATIVITY &
WRITING

ROBERT D.

RICHARDSON,

series editor

A Brighter Word Than Bright

Keats at Work

DAN BEACHY-QUICK

UNIVERSITY
OF IOWA PRESS,
IOWA CITY

University of Iowa Press, Iowa City 52242
Copyright © 2013 by Dan Beachy-Quick
www.uiowapress.org
Printed in the United States of America

Design by Richard Hendel

The University of Iowa Press is a member
of Green Press Initiative and is committed
to preserving natural resources.

Printed on acid-free paper

Library of Congress Cataloging-in-Publication Data
Beachy-Quick, Dan, 1973–
A brighter word than bright: Keats at work /
by Dan Beachy-Quick.
pages cm. — (Muse Books: The Iowa Series in
Creativity and Writing)
Includes bibliographical references and index.
ISBN: 978-1-60938-184-4 (cloth)
ISBN: 978-1-60938-339-8 (paper)
ISBN: 978-1-60938-204-9 (ebook)
1. Keats, John, 1795–1821 — Criticism and interpretation.
2. Poetics. I. Title.
PR4837.B43 2013
821'.7 — dc23   2013005214

For KRISTY, HANA *&* IRIS

cloudy symbols and fever's balm

ACKNOWLEDGMENTS

I owe many people a debt of thanks in the writing of this book; without them it wouldn't have been written. Joseph Parsons first approached me to ask if I'd be interested in working on the Muse Series, and when I answered "Yes, if Keats," he was all encouragement. I am very lucky to find myself surrounded by colleagues who both support and inspire: thank you, Ann Gill, Bruce Ronda, Louann Reid, Mike Lundblad, Matthew Cooperman, and Sasha Steensen. Three friends, all poets, read the entirety of the manuscript, sometimes more than once, and this book is better because of their insights and questions. Thank you, Srikanth Reddy, Sally Keith, and Martin Corless-Smith. I'd like to thank everyone at Iowa University Press, especially Elisabeth Chretien. Thank you to the Muse Series editor, Robert D. Richardson, whose own work has often been my guide. Without the support of a Faculty Development Award from Colorado State University's College of Liberal Arts this book would not have been completed. Thank you to Amy Wright at *Zone 3* for publishing "Portrait: Of His Hand." Lastly, thank you to my children, Hana and Iris, who are daily reminders of uncertainty's wonders, and to my wife, Kristy, who helps make of this life a place where "unbelief has not a space to breathe."

CONTENTS

Again and again, in eternal return, the old orders will not
behave themselves, but move to speak in the new.
—ROBERT DUNCAN, *The H.D. Book*

Keats must get to himself again Severn, if but for us—
I for one cannot afford to lose him—if I kno what it is
to love—I truly love John Keats—
—WILLIAM HASLAM TO JOSEPH SEVERN,
    4 December 1820

If he still cannot bear this, tell him—tell that great poet
and noble-hearted man that we shall all bear his memory in
the most precious part of our hearts, and that the world shall
bow their heads to it as our loves do. Or if this . . . will trouble his
spirit, tell him that we shall never cease to remember and love him,
and that, Christian or Infidel, the most skeptical of us has faith
enough in the high things that nature puts into our heads, to think
that all who are of one accord in mind or heart are journeying to
one and the same place and shall meet somehow or other again,
face to face, mutually conscious, mutually delighted. Tell him he is
only before us on the road, as he was in everything else; or whether
you tell him the latter or no, tell him the former, and add, that we
shall never forget that he was so, and that we are coming after him.
—LEIGH HUNT TO JOSEPH SEVERN, 8 March 1821
    (written two weeks after Keats's death, a fact not yet
    known to him)

In December 1817, the painter B. R. Haydon makes a life-mask of Keats's face—one of the few accurate likenesses in posterity's hands.[1] Haydon will use the likeness to add Keats's profile into his painting "Christ's Entry into Jerusalem," a fact over which Keats, typically (but eerily prescient), jokes: "I have conned over every head in Haydon's Picture. You must warn them not to be afraid should my ghost visit them on Wednesday."[2] Over the course of the next months, on into years, this replica of Keats's face gains a life apart from the poet's own. Leigh Hunt and Benjamin Bailey received Haydon's promise that a replica of the mask would soon be sent their way, though the countenance never arrived. In his letters, Keats asks after his own face, pursues his own likeness, tries to trace his own untraceable image. Keats makes light of it, but behind the ludicrous quality of the problem, there lurks some haunting, telling significance.

One could say of the young poet—the one vaulting in ambition, the one who wants to be included among the immortals of the art he'd practice—that he is one whose voice is in search of his face. Such is the condition of a poet whose stake in the art includes the antique notions of inspiration and genius and soul as absolute necessities. That voice that sings the poems cannot be assumed to be some innate, inner quality. There is, instead, a work to be done—an opening no less difficult for the poet to create than it is for the tight-budded bloom to grow full-blown. The voice must find the face; the face gathers around the voice. Such are the vague, wild emotions, fulgurant within the poet's archetypal word of invocation, cry of pain and cry of joy, earth-shape and zero's rictus, the shape the mouth holds as it sings out: O! —

In a verse letter of 1816 written to his friend Charles Cowden Clarke (musician, son of Keats's schoolmaster, and the person most responsible for introducing Keats to poetry), the young, would-be poet writes:

> Whene'er I venture on the stream of rhyme;
> With shatter'd boat, oar snapt, and canvass rent,
> I slowly sail, scarce knowing my intent;
> Still scooping up the water with my fingers;
> In which a trembling diamond never lingers.[3]

In this image, so early in Keats's experiment in poetry, one can see, can feel, that poetic intent will become that which must be abandoned rather than relied upon. Intent is the spar that poetry shatters; intent is the splintered rudder, leaving the poet with no resource but a broken craft on the swiftly mined stream. The poet finds his hand empty, hanging over the gunwale, fingers dipping down into the water — not to impel and not to steer, but as in a desperate indolence — having failed to capture those trembling diamonds. But those diamonds gleam only on the surface, an ideal wealth or a tantalizing illusion, a trick of the sun, yes — but a diamond to Keats nonetheless. These diamonds tremble. They aren't earth's hardest matter, but are transformed by the poet's own ardent nature; not gem, but the jewel-like quality of how a loved one's fingers might, in sleep, grow tremulous as the dreamer dreams. These diamonds — they are an erotic value, an ideal promise. How can the poet help but ask, *How far into the depths must I reach in order to grasp that which seems at hand?* The eye holds the treasure that leaves the hand bereft. There are the diamonds on the stream; not deep underwater, but deep in the mind — and looking over the edge of the boat, the poet must reach through his own face to collect them.

Keats abandoned his epic poem *Hyperion*, overwhelmed, it seems, not only by the Miltonic echoes in his own work, but more profoundly by his reading of Dante that under-girded his conception of the project.[4] The tale itself, the fall of the Titanic gods as they are overpowered and over-awed by the Olympians, bears in it a parallel to Keats's own efforts in relation to the colossal figures preceding him in English letters. He writes sympathetically, ferocious in his sympathy, of those fallen gods. He would seem to see as broken Oceanus sees, when that old god describes the moment of first beholding Neptune:

> I saw him on the calmed waters scud,
> With such glow of beauty in his eyes,
> That it enforc'd me to bid sad farewell
> To all my empire

It may be truer to say, and more troubling, that Keats sees some version of himself through Oceanus's eyes. He finds himself at a point of poetic awakening — a feeling of utmost power cut always by doubt's swift undercurrent. He finds himself not at that supposed moment every poet strives for, "finding his voice." No, no. He finds himself where we so often find him, at that moment when his voice finds him.

We find him where Mnemosyne, mother of the Muses and memory's embodiment, finds Apollo, whose "enkin-dled" eyes are yet without the song that sparks in them their flame:

> Soon wild commotions shook him, and made flush
> All the immortal fairness of his limbs;
> Most like the struggle at the gate of death;
> Or liker still to one who should take leave
> Of pale immortal death, and with a pang
> As hot as death's is chill, with fierce convulse
> Die into life: so young Apollo anguish'd.[5]

There is the poet-god, peerless in beauty, waking not to
light, but to song which arrives in the throat singing its own
life, buzz of the bee deep in the foxglove, whose sting thrills
words into music.

There is the voice as it finds the poet.

We might find ourselves asking of Keats, as Oceanus asks
of Neptune — we might find ourselves asking as Keats does
after his own life-mask meandering from hand to hand —:

Have ye beheld the young God of the Seas,
My dispossessor? Have ye seen his face?[6]

A NOTE ON THE BOOK

The biographer's art takes a face we thought we clearly knew and, in adjusting the reader's focal distance, reveals to us the blurriness we mistook for fact. Book after book adds to this sum of knowledge, an indelible gift that etches the poet's portrait into ever-firmer lines. But with John Keats, a poet reticent to tell his own friends the facts of his history, accuracy itself falls under scrutiny. The face another gives us, that construction of another's utmost care or spontaneous whim — ranging from the great biographies to Charles Brown's quick sketch of Keats, hand pressed to cheek, gazing off and upward — cannot help but become a mask the next effort tries to revise by removing. I should admit I have little interest in offering a portrait of Keats more accurate than those already available; nor am I capable of doing so. I am more concerned with returning Keats, as best I can manage, back into that half-light that obscures accurate rendering so as to make more brilliant those sudden flashes in his poems and letters that, lightning-like, reveal the storm-tossed grasses in the ceaseless field even as darkness closes the vision again — sudden clarities, and the afterimage that lingers long past the lightning's strike.

This book's effort is to mine Keats's poetic concerns even as it mimics the same. It proceeds by two commingling methods: a set of portraits that privilege allegorical accuracy within a biographical frame, and a chronological reading of Keats's poems and letters, from 1816 to 1820, attending to the ways in which singular concerns grow adhesive, alter, and confound themselves as the man matures into the poet. Keats writes, "Now it appears to me that almost any Man may like the Spider spin from his own inwards his own airy Citadel. The points of leaves and twigs on which the Spider begins her work are few and she fills the Air with a beautiful circuiting."[1] Perhaps the primary crisis of the poet involves taking that which is inward and finding for that structure outward expression. That web-like construction connects together separate points, makes of intervening absence a place of consideration—the cost of thinking is entering; the danger of entering, being trapped. Each thread pulled on exerts a pressure on the whole, as nerve does to body, as nerve does to mind. To exert too much force in one's inquiry risks tearing the web apart. This book is not a work of criticism, but a "tribute and a study."[2] The challenge is, as Robert Duncan puts it as he pays tribute to H.D. in his study of her, a semi-magical one, in which "a spell [may] be felt to be necessary to the works here, for weaving *is* necessary as I go, to keep many threads and many figures so that every thread is central and every figure central to threads and figures, with none coming to conclusion but leading further into the process."[3] Further into the process takes us into the silken threads of Keats's letters and poems, and every point of concern tugs on one such thread so that the whole web thrills in response. The image may be justly accused of being "romantic" in the worst sense, but I cannot help but see, when I imagine Keats's "airy citadel," that what breath blows through it alters its shape, bends it to an inspiration it cannot control, and in that constant re-shaping, Keats's face in its continuous mutability gains its truest form, uncertainly visible from moment to moment, never growing still, changeless only in its change. Such a portrait is the only one Keats has left of himself. It is a drawing done with words and in mystery, brilliant and occult, and it is only by schooling ourselves in such a text, one requiring of us both the difficulty of devotion and devotion to difficulty, that we can learn to read that name "writ in water." How does one do so? One traces the letters as they're written in the element of their own erasure.

Young Keats, Weeping Beneath the Desk

Keats's prodigal mother returned to the family when he was an adolescent; his father had died in a riding accident when he was eight. His mother returned, but returned consumptive. Keats took it upon himself to nurse her, this mother whose impulsiveness, whose enthusiasm, he himself so deeply shared and was shaped by. He would hardly let another person give her medicine, so vigilant was he in his duty.

When he returned to school, summer being over, he had hopes his mother would recover. Such was not the case. When the news came, young Keats — too young yet to have any sense of himself as a poet, but in whom the *Poet* already dwelled — was devastated. This boy who had earned the acceptance of others by being able to beat them into admiration, this fighter, this scrapper, went to the master's desk and bent down underneath it, from which darkness the other boys wept to hear Keats weeping.

The darkness underneath that desk didn't mask his grief, but gave it a maternal housing, as if one could return to the womb of the mother forever gone, and there bewail the terrible fact. The young man crying beneath the desk, weeping there in that darkness, the close-chambers making the sound of his own sorrow echo around him there in that cave underneath the desk's top, becomes for us looking backward an allegorical portrait. The dark enclosure mimics the womb, and in ways the boy could not yet fathom in his grief, his weeping below the desk prefigures a rebirth in which the man will sit before it and write those poems whose long concerns include what the relation of a mortal life is to beings immortal. That desk becomes for the *Poet* in Keats the solid symbol of all the boy has lost; it marks, too, what he will become. The accurate portrait isn't the boy crying; that boy is hidden. It is a trespass to seek him there, though his schoolmates could hear the echoing sobs, and so, perhaps, can we. The portrait is the desk itself, where forever in the cloistered dark a bereft boy weeps, where in the room's light sit pen and ink and a sheaf of paper waiting to be darkened into song. The portrait is not only the desk, but the classroom; and the building in which the classroom sits, whose front of "the purest red brick" that is "wrought by means of moulds into rich designs of flowers and pomegranates, with heads of cherubim over niches"[1] marks the first bower in which the young Keats finds his mind enclosed.

Let us say that the reader, like the spider, has many eyes. Those eyes see not only that which is immediate, but that which reveals itself only in hindsight, only in time past, and sees that past as immediate, as present. Let's say the reader is a spider with eyes symbolic. Those eyes see the young Keats mourning in the desk's dark cavern; those eyes also see the mature Keats reading at a desk, writing at a desk; those eyes also see that the grief-stricken child, and the poet gleaning from his mind the poem, do the same work at the same time. Some music sobs up into song. Some song digs down and confronts what it also must comfort.

1816

Muse

Each morning the Muses sing; in their song, it's always morning. They sing of time, but do not sing *in* it. Hesiod begins his *Theogony* in their invocation:

> I begin my song with the Helikonian Muses;
> they have made Helikon, the great god-haunted
>   mountain, their domain;
> their soft feet move in the dance that rings
> the violet-dark spring and the altar of mighty Zeus.
> They bathe their lithe bodies in the water of Permessos
> or of Hippokrene or of god-haunted Olmeios.
> On Helikon's peak they join hands in lovely dances
> and their pounding feet awaken desire.
> From there they set out and, veiled in mist,
> glide through the night and raise enchanting voices . . .
> It was they who taught Hesiod beautiful song
> As he tended his sheep at the foothills of god-haunted
>   Helikon.[1]

The Muses sing, each day they sing, the story of the creation of the world entire, and sing of those gods whose powers riddle and haunt the world still. The Muses teach the poet his song as he tends his sheep. Perhaps he overhears what is not his to hear, and his own song seeks forgiveness for that trespass even as it seeks recognition; perhaps his mind grew inspired when from his duty he grew distracted, noting the bees so punctual to the waiting clover.

The Muses sometimes "bathe their lithe bodies" in the Hippocrene, that same fountain Keats will—mired so in time, but so heedless of its chain—wish for a "blushful" beaker of to quicken again the dull ache of his numb heart back into inspired life. Keats thirsts for the presence of the Muses. Thirst includes desire, requires it. To awaken to the song the Muses sing is also to "awaken desire" within oneself, and the poet who can hear the god-haunted song the Muses sing finds himself haunted—for desire is a kind of haunting. The desire-haunted poet is one who is capable not only of reaching Helicon's heights, but also of being led astray, following not the Muses as they return up the mountain, but tracing through the gloom those muse-like others who, not singing themselves, create in the poet desire that sings.

Keats feels the threat inside desire's promise — or is it the promise inside desire's threat? — from the onset of his writing poems. In one of his earliest lyrics he writes:

> Fill for me a brimming bowl,
> And let me in it drown my soul:
> But put therein some drug design'd
> To banish Woman from my mind.
> For I want not the stream inspiring,
> That heats the sense with lewd desiring;
> But I want as deep a draught
> As e'er from Lethe's waves was quaft,
> From my despairing breast to charm
> The image of the fairest form
> That e'er my rev'ling eyes beheld,
> That e'er my wand'ring fancy spell'd![2]

From the earliest poems, Keats feels a crisis within desire — a schism that complicates the very notion of creative work. The poem demands an erotic effort that mimics love's own nature: that it become a desire-haunted region whose end isn't arrival so much as it is pursuit. Love requires lack, that sense of want that makes the one desired not simply a kind of attraction, but more deeply, an existential pull: it is exactly she who seems to promise to fill what in the self is lacking. To "banish Woman from my mind" only deepens that lack, one that requires Lethe's draught so as to forget desire's damage—making emptiness emptier, lack more lacking—and forgetfulness becomes Love's paradoxical realm, where one can observe who one wants without the pain of wanting her. Keats predicts for himself a difficulty from whose Gordian knot he'll never remove himself: he wants to "banish Woman from my mind" only to behold her once again before his "rev'ling eyes." Keats wants the mind's own imaginative matter to leap through forgetfulness back into being, and so by his own forgetfulness—of self and self-history and self-want—return pure, essential, whole. But the Poet in Keats is too deeply attuned to desire's music to believe that any wanting can purify itself of its own erotic nature—a nature that knows that self and other must trespass, must intermingle, must rupture the minor reality of any single self in order to dwell in the more dubious, consummate world. This sense of being is in its very nature desirous and instilling of desire, witness to the erotic other in all her otherness. Hers is also, almost always, an otherness embedded in the mind of the one who loves: the poet, who finds trapped in his mind the image of the lovely being who traps him. It is hard work to be under the spell of the Muse.

Muse

When Keats gives Clarke a group of poems to show Leigh Hunt, he seems a little abashed that "the Muse is so frequently mentioned."[3] Almost all of the poems of the time are addressed to a Muse, only some of them Helicon's immortal goddesses. He writes sonnets in honor of those whose company he soon will keep: Hunt, Haydon, Clarke, and his brothers Tom and George. He writes sonnets to those poets he most admires: Wordsworth, Chatterton, Byron, Milton, Spenser. He sings back to Apollo Apollo's own song. Keats calls out to the muses near at hand as fervently as he calls back to the Muses of the old, ongoing world. Those worlds — the Hunt circle, his brothers, and the god-haunted mountains — are not separate worlds for Keats, though it would be foolish to call them one. Keats feels the mythic underlay to life's daily surface, and the poems begin, as soon as he devotes himself to the writing of them, to seek ways to draw those worlds into their curious consummation. Keats knows this himself, knows it keenly. He writes to Clarke in a verse letter:

> The air that floated by me seem'd to say,
> "Write! thou wilt never have a better day."
> And so I did. When many lines I'd written,
> Though with their grace I was not oversmitten,
> Yet, as my hand was warm, I thought I'd better
> Trust to my feelings, and write you a letter.
> Such an attempt required an inspiration
> Of a peculiar sort, — a consummation; —[4]

The poem is that consummation — the page beneath the words a place of erotic potency, where creative expression reaches completion not in the poet's final utterance, but in the creative reception of the listening other whose attention commingles two minds into one. The poem becomes a work that affirms two lives genuinely intermingled at the very place that mingling occurs. For Clarke and Keats, that place was Clarke's home, where they "revel'd in a chat that ceased not / When at night-fall among your books we got."[5] And those feelings to which Keats trusts are feelings more precise than concepts allow; they are the very stuff of the nerves inspired. For Clarke would walk Keats halfway back to the house where the young man apprenticed to a country doctor; they would shake hands, and then Clarke would return. Keats would listen, he says, to the footsteps until they disappeared. But wait—they haven't disappeared. The Muses have brought him a song through the air, a strange song, but real. Clarke walks on, heard once again through the fact of that silence slowly enveloping him: "You chang'd the footpath for the grassy plain."[6] The foot in the grass is another song, a quieter one, as the Muse of the bent grass knows, than the foot on the hard, weary road; and Keats does not turn homeward until he hears it.

Silence

1.

Not only laden with the full-blown flower's scent, the air hums with bees in flight, wending their way from bloom to bloom.

> What is more soothing than the pretty hummer
> That stays one moment in an open flower,
> And buzzes cheerily from bower to bower?[7]

To imagine fully the world of Keats's poem, a reader must hear the steady drone of the bee's wings in flight. That hum hums beneath many of the poems, predicts the later gnats and their "mournful wail," creates a drone so steady it ceases to be heard even as it is ever present, so ever present it seems almost like silence — a silence one hears.

2.

In classical Indian music, the tambura produces a buzzing drone against which the melody of the raga plays. The drone is present to create the silence needed for the melody to be heard, as if a creative silence must be created within a silence of negation, a blank that does not deny the world, but makes it possible.

3.

Radio telescopes pick up from the very edge of the universe in every direction the earliest evidence of the universe's *agony*, its coming into being. It sounds like a steady, static buzz. When astronomers add computer-generated color to the finding, the whole universe is surrounded by a creamy beige the color of old, thick paper.

4.

Keats creates within his poems a drone, often bees, sometimes gnats. The drone is not limited to sound. Flowers
scent the air unceasingly. The violent critical reaction of
Keats's own time to the "Cockney" influence in the poems,
their overabundant luxury, failed to see the deep neces-
sity of such sensory saturation. Less virulent forms of the
same criticism persist today, a steady stream of dismissing
the early poems as the young poet's failing, if still needed,
experiments. Such critiques mistake depth for shallowness,
mistake a young poet forging the phenomenological base of
his poetic for "style." Incipient in Keats, even now in 1816,
is the sense that a poem founds a world it also finds. The
poem is that world, formed of words and which words reveal. For a word to be heard, it needs silence. To exist, such
silence must be heard, must also be created. Keats creates
such silence; such silence is the first creative act, and the
poems must include in them their own origin, the nothing against which something occurs. This singing silence,
this silence that presents itself, comes to greater and greater
concern as Keats writes into the fullness of his power. At
greatest crisis, this silence becomes silent itself. That silence
is the Grecian Urn.

Sometimes I think a poetic presses down upon the poet's mind as does a seal upon the soft wax that closes a letter. Sometimes I think it takes a lifetime for the seal to press down, and with every poem, year after year, the impression presses deeper. The early poems in a poet's life show the shallow edges of a concern that in the last poems will be deeply marked.

That poetic seal promises other meanings. The image on the seal closes from view those words meant only for the recipient's eyes. The image faces all who hold the letter, a public value. But the image keeps secret other words, a sacred value.

It is worth noting that the waxen image must be broken for the letter to be read.

Keats writes two poems to his brother George, one a sonnet and one of much greater length. In both, the young poet expresses — almost naively, so strenuous is their enthusiasm — certain poetic ideals that will only deepen over the course of the coming years. In the sonnet, he writes:

> E'en now, dear George, while this for you I write,
>   Cynthia is from her silken curtains peeping
> So scantly, that it seems her bridal night,
>   And she her half-discover'd revels keeping.
> But what, without the social thought of thee,
> Would be the wonders of the sky and sea?[8]

Keats wants his brother to know that he has witnessed the goddess even as she discovers the secret of her bridal night. To interpret the image simply as a metaphor of romantic fancy is to dismiss its devotion to imagination's fevered transport. Keats can see, he says, through those veils that keep the moon merely the moon. His work vaults him into sacred glimpses, and the work of the poem is to show how the sacred might show itself forth within the confines of the profane world, how the moon can be moon and Cynthia at once. We see the sacred discovering a secret, Cynthia's "half-discover'd revels" of her bridal night. It is a strange thing to suggest, that there is that which the goddess must herself discover — it is as if in her peering out the curtains, the moon peering out the scant clouds, she steps out of her own godly capacity, omniscience gently dropped away as a wedding dress drops away, to discover what can be found in no other way: the revels of the bridal chamber.

It seems past human nature to turn one's eyes away just as the goddess appears, but Keats does. He says there are no "wonders of the sky and sea" without the "social thought" of his brother. The couplet values the profane, and so the sacred retreats, and the poem ends. But such dichotomy dissatisfies reader and poet both. In the longer poem, Keats returns to similar imagery to speak more confoundingly of his aspiration (an aspiration perhaps only discovered by the writing of the poem that expresses it, and so explanatory of the need to unfold the sonnet's brevity into the later poem's extent):

> The sage will mingle with each moral theme
> My happy thoughts sententious; he will teem
> With lofty periods when my verses fire him,
> And then I'll stoop from heaven to inspire him.
> Lays have I left of such a dear delight
> That maids will sing them on their bridal night.[9]

Keats has exchanged places with the moon. Now he is at height, the atmosphere ethereal his verse has cast him up to, and his own song descends to give melody and words to maidens on their wedding night. The conditions of the sonnet find themselves reversed, and no longer is Keats choosing the social over the sacred. He is seeking instead a way to intertwine opposed realities. Cynthia's wedding night and the earthly maiden's similar revels would all sing the same song. It is the very song that ties them together.

Genius

Genius has an appetite; it wants to eat the world.

Keats knows a poet forms a world when a poet writes a poem. Later, he will know that world must come "as naturally as the Leaves to a tree [or] it had better not come at all."[10] But the earliest imprint of organic form confuses world and poem, confounds mouth and ear, entwines self and other. Such work seeks the genuine, and so explores genius:

> Much have I travell'd in the realms of gold,
>   And many goodly states and kingdoms seen;
>   Round many western islands have I been
> Which bards in fealty to Apollo hold.
> Oft of one wide expanse had I been told
>   That deep-brow'd Homer ruled as his demesne;
>   Yet did I never breathe its pure serene
> Till I heard Chapman speak out loud and bold[11]

Rumor is a gossipy wind. It pushes the sail in the mind toward an island charted on every map but sighted by none. Reading is an intrepid, leaky craft, seeking among the depthless wilds those "western islands" poets form. Journey breathes differently than arrival. Keats finds in Chapman's Homer, read out loud through the night with Clarke, an arrival at inspiration. The notion alters our assumptions about it. Inspiration is breath confused with appetite, breath grown substantial, and the source of that breath is another's breathing. Homer's breath is the very wind of the world that pushed Odysseus's ship astray for its years of homeless wandering. To breathe in that world is to consume it, and by consuming, conserve it.

Part of such conservation is Keats's need to write a poem to mark the discovery; such work is ingenious. It must recognize the other by conducting a work of its own, an act that makes hazy the distinction between sacrifice and gift. That haziness is genius's own lovely obscurity. In the ancient sense, genius referred to that god which, at the very moment of our birth, protected our life. The cake we eat on our birthday has as its origins a bloodless sacrifice to the god of genius dwelling within us—the satisfaction of our own sweet tooth is happy accident to ancient obedience. When confused, we touch the center of our forehead, right there where genius is rumored to dwell, a little other in the very midst of self. To listen to genius is to let oneself be guided by that voice in the self that is not the self's own. It implies an otherness exactly where we expect to find identity; it speaks within us a rumor to us, that we are least ourselves where we are most ourselves. A guide that misdirects, genius orients us always back out of the self as sufficient confine, disables the ease of our self-sufficiency. Our genius locates our most essential self outside of the boundaries we normally claim by saying "I." It is not so much our recognition of the impersonal, but the impersonal's recognition of us. That difference, once established, is vast, is filled with "wild surmise,"[12] for it undermines the hierarchy of self to genius, and makes one possessed instead of possessing. The self given over to genius is always more than and less than itself, never merely itself. Genius undermines lesser forms of completion by making the self both less than and more than itself, by altering one's relation to oneself so that Heraclitus's fragment, "too much and never enough,"[13] becomes curiously self-defining. Genius instills in the self that listens to it a form of desire that, the more its appetite is fed, only grows more desirous. Such an appetite breathes in another's poem (as here, Chapman's Homer), reading as an act of consumption. The end isn't satiety, but the need to create another poem.

In this sense, one could talk of genius as a digestive activity—and indeed, genius oversees those functions the conscious mind seeks no control over, lest in gaining it, we die: heartbeat, appetite, digestion, breath. When, in the next year, Keats writes to Reynolds, "I find that I cannot exist without poetry, without eternal poetry;"[14] he is speaking of what he has discovered in the sonnets and other poems of 1816. He is not joking, nor is he euphemizing. He has discovered he is hungry; he has discovered he must be fed. There is that genius in him which, being eternal itself, must be fed by eternal food. Keats learns not to read Homer, but to inhale him. The old gods, it's said, could feed upon the fumes of the sacrifices burnt for them; so genius lives on words, and the ancient breath words contain, the very breath of the poet himself. Keats gives us the lines that mark the fervor of his appetency:

> How many bards gild the lapses of time!
>> A few of them have ever been the food
>> Of my delighted fancy[15]

Imagination, so it seems, like the body itself, suffers appetite, and in its hunger is its delight. Keats not only marks the lines of his appetite, he gives us the very image of what such hungering looks like, not an image of himself, but an image of another, genius's own portrait:

> Haply 'tis when thy ruby lips part sweetly,
>> And so remain, because thou listenest[16]

Genius listens with parted lips.

Inspiration

The air carries on it the scent of flowers, as if the inspiring breeze is inspired itself. Keats, throughout his poetry, is aware of such burdens, if perfume can be a burden to what carries it. Air also carries the bee's hum, the bird's music. "What is more tranquil than a musk-rose blowing / In a green island, far from all men's knowing?," Keats writes in the opening of "Sleep and Poetry," making of "blowing" a gentle pun implying both the musk-rose's full blossoming and the air that blows the flower's scent to the poet. Such "blowing" is far from "knowing," is no fact of mere witness, but a deeper fact, one that can be known only by being experienced. To experience it, breathe in; and the eye, too, sees by breathing into the mind what's in front of it. The air — we forget it, but Keats realizes and realizes it again — is a medium. It is blank as the page is blank, but a blanker form of blank, inscribed not with words but the world's own sense — odor and sound and light — that across unmeasured distance speaks of that which exists, but exists elsewhere. "[A]ll the secrets of some wond'rous thing / . . . breathes about us in the vacant air."[17] The poet breathes in, closes his eyes and breathes in, and finds in the mind's bower the musk-rose full blown, and the air "[s]ometimes . . . gives a glory to the voice."[18]

"Air" itself is a pun: music and breath as well as what wind pushes through; nor is it far to *pneuma* and *spirit*, so that air becomes a strange sort of soul, outside every body but into every body breathed, carrying on it the old voices just as it carries a rose's scent, so that the poet is one who might "echo back the voice of thine own tongue"[19] in order to write a poem. Sometimes that voice is poppy laden, and to listen is to fall asleep. Keats breathes in just such a voice, finds himself desperate to do so — not to know, for knowing in any typical sense is not Keats's concern. He seeks a glimpse exactly of what he cannot know, would not know, but would be in presence of. The cost of such poetic desire baffles itself with itself, and in "Sleep and Poetry," Keats expresses this desire that will wend its way through the major poems to come, poems in the air, even now, as he breathes in and so falls asleep. He must. The sleeping mind unfolds into its other waking where the scent of the rose unfolds in the mind, present in the space of knowing, but a presence that cannot be known—imagination being, like the air, a thing that is also a nothing, real but ungraspable, frustrating knowing with a refusal to exist in knowledge, frustrating philosophy by refusing to not exist.

Inspiration initiates Keats into imagination, and imagination initiates Keats into death:

> . . . yet, to my ardent prayer,
> Yield from thy sanctuary some clear air,
> Smoothed for intoxication by the breath
> Of flowering bays, that I may die a death
> Of luxury, and my young spirit follow
> The morning sun-beams to the great Apollo
> Like a fresh sacrifice; or, if I can bear
> The o'erwhelming sweets, 'twill bring to me the fair
> Visions of all places: a bowery nook
> Will be elysium—an eternal book
> Whence I may copy many a lovely saying
> About the leaves, and flowers—[20]

Imagination is a sacrificial rite. To imagine is to find oneself on the altar. Sleep allows us to continue to experience the world without the world falling into experience, experience into recognition, recognition into knowledge, and knowledge into that dull idea of the world which needs no senses to be in it. Keats gains as a poetic truth something that will later, in such heartbreaking ways, become a mortal truth. Death lives inside us. The poet—as the hero must on a quest — enters the underworld, the afterlife, in order to find that world that never passes out of itself, the unceasing world. Consciousness is a myth. Keats seeks such consciousness; the poems are the very evidence of the effort. In this Elysium, this death within the self to which the self must be sacrificed, one finds those already written words "about the leaves, and flowers." To copy down such words, and to move toward waking — that reemergence from death itself that is the hero's other task — is to return not with an image in any normal sense of the word. That mere work denies the old superstition that word and world are coexistent. The task is to arrive with a word written on a page — say it is "musk-rose" — which, read properly, is inhaled, for the word is the very bloom. As Keats knows, to wake from such deathly effort is to lose that Elysium, but not to lose it entirely. It exists in us as does a dream when we wake, continuing its work in the dark in us. But such visions come with necessary consequence, ethical and aesthetical both:

> The visions all are fled — the car is fled
> Into the light of heaven, and in their stead
> A sense of real things comes doubly strong[21]

Death doubles the reality of the world when we return to reality. The poem on the page — the poem on the air of the page — is evidence of this doubled world.

Imagination

Imagination spells the world; the world spells imagination. World also dispels imagination; and by imagination, world is dispelled. At times, in the poems of 1816, imagination shepherds the poet away from the busy world's "little cares," and we encounter early and often those bowers in which Keats or his heroes will seek that curious form of rest that unfolds into imaginative experience, be it dream or be it book:

> To one who has been long in city pent,
>   'Tis very sweet to look into the fair
>   And open face of heaven, — to breathe a prayer
> Full in the smile of the blue firmament.
> Who is more happy, when, with heart's content,
>   Fatigued he sinks into some pleasant lair
>   Of wavy grass, and reads a debonair
> And gentle tale of love and languishment?[22]

Keats finds a place within the world to lose the world entire. Imagination pulls the mind into that "gentle tale" of which the grave trivialities of the city deny entrance. To open a book is to find not a word-printed page, but a window carelessly left open through which the reader steps, seeking to be excused from reality in order to land in a world that seems, impossibly, more than real. The enchantment lingers about the senses even when the book is closed.

> Returning home at evening, with an ear
>   Catching the notes of Philomel, — an eye
> Watching the sailing cloudlet's bright career,
>   He mourns that day so soon has glided by[23]

His foray into the "gentle tale of love and languishment," this mind's beguilement, this imagination's spell, conducts a secret work on the poet. His senses seem heightened; they also seem altered. His senses seem altered; they also seem altering. The page closed within the book continues to exist in the mind, so that the nightingale's song isn't merely the drab thrush singing unseen from the brush, the cloud does not merely move through the sky as the wind pushes it, no; the singing nightingale is Philomela transformed, and the cloud is ship all gallant. Imagination spells the eye as the eye sees the world, enchants the ear into hearing not what is in the air to hear, but to hear within the bird's song another world impossibly present, the god-haunted world of myth. Imagination twines that world — real but nowhere graspable, present everywhere but nowhere discernable — with this world, in which a thrush sings amid the city's noise. Imagination lets the senses themselves grow sensible. The eye sees that it sees; the ear hears that it hears; and the figure of consciousness multiplies "I think, therefore I am" into a figure of Typhonic complications. Imagination turns *I* into *many*, a difficult gift embedded in Keats's poetic efforts from the first poems he wrote.

Imagination also contains within it a secret mourning: the "day . . . has glided by." Keats senses that all he has gained by reading his "gentle tale" has also divorced him from the live-long day. The page spelled him a world that dispelled a world, and though he can hear Philomela sing, something in him realizes, worries, mourns, that he can no longer hear the modest bird's lovely song as merely what it is: a bird's lovely song.

He knows he is *spelled* — the word appears strangely often in the early poems. Speaking of a gift from a friend, flowers sent in apology over a minor spat, Keats writes: "O Wells! thy roses came to me / My sense with their deliciousness was spell'd."[24] Not only words can enchant, but the world itself can do so, the very things of the world. In "Oh! how I love, on a fair summer's eve," when he takes imaginative leave from "meaner thoughts" and "little cares," he finds himself "musing on Milton's fate" until the epic poet's "stern form" acts upon him as "when some melodious sorrow spells mine eyes." Milton's sternness fascinates, for it not only seems descriptive of the poet, but contains within it a demand to think back to the world, to dispel the vision, to return from enchantment's thrall. The image gains a life outside the mind, and then acts against the mind that birthed it.

Imagination contains within it some ethical crisis. Its spell spells it out. Through words one gains a world. That world is mythic, eternal, *of* time but not *in* time. One does not live in it, not exactly. Nothing here is exact. One finds this world within oneself even as one wakes to find oneself in it. To be under the spell is to admit — at times fearfully, at times audaciously — that one doesn't know the line that marks the boundary between the actual world and the imagined one. The spelled mind is devoted to those moments in which reality complicates itself with what normally would by the world be excluded; it suspects the image enchants precisely because it is real, and the image of the rose is as real as the musk-rose, is as real as that rose's scent inhaled, and the image has its bouquet, too.

How to smell the rose that isn't there? That rose on the page? That many-worded rose, more petal-words than petals? You allow the world its vagrancy. Words are a vagrant work. Then thought is but one of those tendrils that holds the whole together, and to imagine affirms an aspect of the world that can be affirmed in no other way. Imagination then acts as does the "long grass which hems / A little brook."[25] It keeps the whole together. Or it might. "Hem" is such a curious word, evocative first of delicate stitching, then invoking that clearing of the throat before one speaks. When the grass speaks, when the wind moves through it, it can sound like a little brook; and the long grass seems hemmed into the very bank. The imagination knows this is true, as does Keats. Pushed to its furthest implication — a thinking Keats will arrive at soon, though now he has but taken his first steps — to imagine the world is to participate in its ongoing creation: it hems the long grass to the little brook, it hems the brook to the little book. Word leads to world. It almost spells it.

Thought

Words are substance strange. Speak one and the air ripples into another's ears. Write one and the eye laps it up. But the sense transmutes, and the spoken word winds through the ear's labyrinth into a sense that is no longer the nerve's realm. The written word unfolds behind the eye into world, world's image, and the imagination sees as the eye cannot see—thoughtfully.

One of Keats's early muses is Solitude, an allegorical figure whose strangeness lends it the feel of a companion even as it offers itself as a region of contemplation. Person and place coincide. In solitude Keats could learn to study "Nature's observatory," but he prefers "the sweet converse of an innocent mind, / Whose words are images of thoughts refin'd."[26] The erotic strand of Keats's poetic concerns is not absent from the other's "innocent mind"; it depends upon it. The innocent mind is the one that can speak so that word and world and thought do not dissolve into those separate threads into which experience demands they unravel. It is a song resistant to the world *as* experience, the world *of* experience; it is a song *before* experience, sung so as to return us to a vision experience seems to deny as ours. To sing so is to see that thinking about the world is to dwell more profoundly in it. The words of the song are likewise those images of the world that are themselves the thoughts they pattern in it. To sing is to be among the sinews, the tendrils, the nervy span.

When Keats, in the same poem, writes from his solitary witness of "where the deer's swift leap / Startles the wild bee from the fox-glove bell"[27] he is not merely describing an action, a cause and a consequence. He writes so as to see lyrically. Lyric vision shies away from logic and its consequences—*if* and *then* don't proscribe a narrative framework; they open a field of interrelation in which simultane-ities undermine consequence. The deer by its leap startling the bee out of the flower is but a single image, an image of how the mind might learn to think, if thinking occurs where word and world coincide, and if the eye is the organ of philosophy.

Beauty

Beauty's curious principle winds intricately between world and mind, stitching the opposites together, thrilling thought with the nervy points that pierce meditation into thralldom. Keats is an apprentice to such beauty. That beauty makes itself evident often in the body of another:

> Light feet, dark violet eyes, and parted hair;
>> Soft dimpled hands, white neck, and creamy breast,
>> Are things on which the dazzled senses rest
> Till the fond, fixed eyes forget they stare.[28]

In Keats's earliest poems, beauty already operates as a principle dismissive of thought's logic. The mind alters in beauty's presence. It can no longer retreat away from the senses into realms where idea reigns, but finds itself instead extending to the very ends of the nerves that remove thought from airless truth and brings thinking back to blood and breath. The eyes stare until they "forget they stare." Beauty disables thinking's premeditation; beauty opens up a field in the mind whose boundaries have no marked edge. The blank gaze waits to see even as it sees, and the dazzled mind waits behind it, wondering but fixed, wandering but enthralled as if to a single point—but it is a point that is also an expanse.

Here, truth is not liberating.

> . . . In truth there is no freeing
> One's thoughts from such a beauty; when I hear
>> A lay that once I saw her hand awake,
> Her form seems floating palpable, and near;
>> Had I e'er seen her from an arbour take
> A dewy flower, oft would that hand appear,
>> And o'er my eyes the trembling moisture shake.[29]

Thought in thralldom caught alters thinking. It puts the mind in the eye and in the ear, in the senses entire. Then a tear is "an intellectual thing."[30] Keats doesn't know, nor is the mind in beauty's midst capable of seeking knowledge. Truth is a cold realm compared to "her hand" he once saw wake a melody. That "lay," that music he recalls her own hand playing, is beauty's phantasm. Keats becomes receptive, for now the mind is as the nerves are, a medium of transfer, not bound to logic's strictures. He can hear a melody so that the image of the woman who once played it for him appears again in his eyes, beauty's tantalizing refusal to obey nature's mere rules, where out of the music the woman steps, harming the mind by disarming it, and fusing into one the dew dropped from the flowers on his eyes, and those tears the young poet might feel gathering, shaken so by the beauty-shattered mind's — not thought — vision.

Eros

An erotic poetics finds itself in continual crisis, demands of the poet strange necessities relieved only in the writing of the poem itself. Erotic crisis not only speaks of the moment, etymologically, when a woman goes into labor, but in stranger ways, speaks of the poet's own labor — not merely the near-cliché of poem as version of child, but the more tormented ground in which the poet must write that erotic ceremony in whose consummation he witnesses his own birth.

An erotic image is no single moment, though Pound seems right to say it occurs in "an instant of time."[31] Zeno might point out that any instant of time is all time together, a kind of eternity temporary only to those who, like us, must live through every instant, and so find ourselves by eternity abandoned. If we can further expand Pound's definition of image, his "intellectual and emotional complex,"[32] into a more Keatsian mythic ground, we find that in the trope of image, Psyche and Cupid reenact the whole story of their love. The human element, call it representation or witness, seeks the eternal element, call it truth or god, and the image in the poem is bridal chamber, erotic bower, and threshing ground all. Psyche wanders through the poems even when we don't recognize her:

> Were I in such a place, I sure should pray
> That nought less sweet might call my thoughts away,
> Than the soft rustle of a maiden's gown
> Fanning away the dandelion's down[33]

Though not yet at the perfection of the goddess Autumn "sitting careless on a granary floor,"[34] this image in "I stood tip-toe upon a little hill" is one facet of the same concern, for the erotic image presents itself as a source that cannot be depleted, a chamber to which the poet must continually learn how to return. The woman's gown fans away the dandelion seeds; the same woman will later need to regather them in order to regain her love.

Keats doesn't seem yet to know this image is an image of Psyche herself, so unconscious is the poem at work in him. But Psyche soon appears, witnessed by the poet whose labor it is to tell the tale of what he sees:

> So felt he, who first told, how Psyche went
> On the smooth wind to realms of wonderment;
> What Psyche felt, and Love, when their full lips
> First touch'd; what amorous, and fondling nips
> They gave each other's cheeks; with all their sighs,
> And how they kist each other's tremulous eyes[35]

If myth is, in part, the ongoing tale of the god's own creation, a creation that can continue to occur only by the tale being told, then an erotic poetics is one that seeks through the poem's own labor an entrance into that creative source. One might think of the erotic as a necessary trespass, a betrayal of the sanctity of the other in order to allow the other to continue to exist. The poem is tense with such contraries: it must see the kiss the eyes must close to receive.

As with Keats's sonnet to his brother George, "I stood tip-toe upon a little hill" wends its ambling way to Cynthia, and to the heartfelt, erotic, desire to witness "thy bridal night!" It is a key wish for Keats, central to the deep work his poetry strives to accomplish. It leads him to an extraordinary question, one that can only be asked by laboring in the erotic crisis of the poem itself. He asks: "Was there a Poet born?" It is a question he is asking about himself.

Apprenticeship

Keats began his medical training at the young age of fourteen, apprenticed to a surgeon in Edmonton, a Mr. Thomas Hammond. He lived in the same house with his mentor, took meals with him, and began his study of anatomy among other, often menial chores. The secret benefit to the placement had little to do with Mr. Hammond himself, but everything to do with the fact that young Keats was only two miles away from Enright, where his older friend Charles Cowden Clarke lived. When Keats found himself free of duty, he would wander over: "He rarely came empty-handed; either he had a book to read, or brought one to be exchanged. When the weather permitted, we always sat in an arbour at the end of a spacious garden, and—in Boswellian dialect—'we had good talk.'"[1]

I like to think about Keats walking those miles, carrying in his hand a book between two houses. In each house, in different but overlapping ways, he was an apprentice. I like to think the lessons of anatomy taxed his imagination in ways that reading poetry both affirmed and complicated. One practice taught him to read so as to see into what the body keeps hidden; the other practice taught him that the body keeps hidden things which are not of the body at all: birds, the singing of birds, beauty and beauty's own world. I like to think of that road Keats walked, the place where both forms of knowledge confounded each other, where seeming opposites—medicine and poetry—ceased to oppose.

Imagination can so radicalize empathy that one can weep for what isn't there.

Clarke remembers:

Once, when reading the "Cymbeline" aloud, I saw his
eyes fill with tears, and his voice faltered when he came
to the departure of Posthumus, and Imogen saying she
would have watched him —
    'Till the diminution
    Of space had pointed him sharp as my needle;
    Nay follow'd him till he had *melted from*
    The smallness of a gnat to air; and then
    Have turn'd mine eye and wept.[2]

It takes but a mile or two for a body to become a needle
and then a gnat. So must Keats have looked to Clarke as
his young friend returned to the house in which he lived,
not yet poetry's bower, but the doctor's office in which the
future poet learned how the blood circulated through the
human heart.

Keats's medical training was far from "modern"; no one had
yet introduced ether into the surgery room. To whatever degree new discoveries had begun to revolutionize the medical profession, there still existed the old beliefs, handed to
young Keats — much as Cowden handed him Shakespeare
and Spenser — from centuries before. In such thinking, the
blood contained humors, and as with consumptive patients,
sometimes the blood would be let to let the bad humor out.
Some bodies produced a "black bile" and such people became Melancholic, given over to fantastic imaginings, erotic
raptures seldom made actual, and profound retreats into
gloom and darkness.[3] Keats in later years suffered from his
"blue demons." Body and mind in such medicine did not
keep themselves separate, but were wholly interpenetrat-
ing, so that Empedocles's old belief that thought was blood
circulating around the human heart was not a poetical error
from ancient times, but a valid medical theory. And as the

mind could find no genuine separation from the body, so the body can find no real distance from the world. As Giorgio Agamben writes: "[T]he breath that animates the universe, circulates in the arteries, and fertilizes the sperm is the same one that, in the brain and in the heart, receives and forms the phantasms of the things we see, imagine, dream, and love."[4] The heart was the center of such spiritual work, this work of soul and breath. The senses press upon the body an image the body stores; the storeroom is the human heart. When an image is evoked—by word or sense of memory or will—the heart releases back into the blood that phantasm of breath that in the mind unfolds again as body, the *imagined* body.[5] Keats learned from medicine, as much as he learned from poetry, the reality of imagination's work. To think, to imagine fully, eclipses the mind's mere bounds, breaks through idea's limited ideal, and affects the body deeply, rigorously, *spiritually*, to its very vital, pulsing point.

At his life's end, Keats and most of his friends thought it was his mind that was killing him.

Severn reports that Keats said to him: "He says that the continued stretch of his imagination has killed him and were he to recover he could not write another line."[6]

Imagination is a fatal work.

Fate requires imagination.

Charles Brown offers this explanation as to why Keats abandoned his medical career:

> He has assured me the muse had no influence over him in his determination, he being compelled, by conscientious motives alone, to quit the profession, upon discovering that he was unfit to perform a surgical operation. He ascribed his inability to an overwrought apprehension of every possible chance of doing evil in the wrong direction of the instrument. "My last operation," he told me,

"was the opening of a man's temporal artery. I did it with the utmost nicety; but, reflecting on what passed through my mind at the time, my dexterity seemed a miracle, and I never took up the lancet again."[7]

Keats could imagine too vividly the damage he had not done to continue doing surgery. So he claimed. But he only failed his apprenticeship in the shallowest sense. His training had never been simply practical, a career earned at the lancet's tip and the needle's suture. Nor can it be said he apprenticed himself to the muse. He apprenticed himself to the imagination's actuality, and that half-lit realm where what is possible is also real.

1817

The Burden of a Shepherd Song

Leigh Hunt, center of the circle of poets that included both Keats and Shelley, lost a tooth as a schoolboy when his teacher threw a copy of Homer's *Iliad* and struck him in the mouth.[1] It may prove no more than a curious overlap, no doubt an accidental one, to note that one of the typical initiatory rites in archaic cultures was the knocking out of a novice's tooth to mark the transition from childhood to adulthood. Accident aside, it seems fair to say that Hunt was initiated into poetic work, and the epic was what struck that initiation home.

Early in 1817, Hunt proposed a challenge to Shelley and Keats—for each to write a long poem, four thousand lines, to be finished at summer's end, the "laurel crown" going to the poet whose verse outpaced the others in accomplishment. Keats escaped London to spend the spring and summer writing *Endymion*. He arrived in Carisbrooke in April, hung portraits of his muses above his bookshelf—Haydon, Mary Queen of Scots, and Milton "with his daughters in a row"—and found in the rented quarters "a head of Shakespeare which I had not before seen."[2] He mused on ambition; he worried ambition might be his Muse. Most of the few poems he wrote before undertaking the full "burden of a shepherd song" revolve around being given a laurel crown by a "young lady," being crowned with laurel by Hunt himself, and being witnessed by two women as Hunt did so. The laurel crown is Apollo's crown, poet-prophet, reminder of his love for Daphne, and Daphne's metamorphosis, which denied him his godly desire. Keats knows it:

> . . . why sit here
> In the sun's eye, and 'gainst my temples press
> Apollo's very leaves—[3]

And in the sonnet to Hunt:

> Minutes are flying swiftly; and as yet
>> Nothing unearthly has enticed my brain
>> Into a delphic labyrinth. I would fain
> Catch an immortal thought to pay the debt
> I owe to the kind poet who has set
>> Upon my ambitious head a glorious gain—
>> Two bending laurel sprigs—'tis nearly pain
> To be conscious of such a coronet.[4]

Wearing the laurel crown creates a crisis in Keats, creates in him a gratitude for a recognition he also feels and fears he does not yet deserve. Such a crown bestowed by Hunt confirms one of young Keats's dearest aspirations: to be a poet among poets. It also awakens him—poignantly, painfully—to the realization that such a crown is not Hunt's to bestow, nor his to wear. Apollo's crown circles the head so as to open it to "immortal thought," not to recognize mere mortal work already accomplished. Keats's "consciousness of such a coronet" describes a painful self-awareness of being unable to lose himself in that "delphic labyrinth" whose very bewilderment signals an arrival within inspiration's maze. If such a crown grows heavy—heavier than two sprigs should allow—it is because the symbol of the crown gains greater reality than its social significance. To be called a poet, and considered so, by Hunt is a social reward, one consequence of which is writing the long poem Keats has been challenged to write. But to wear a laurel crown is also to step into the symbolic, allegoric, role of Poet, one that pushes aside social conventions, or steps through them, and demands vision of another world. Keats feels in himself a responsibility to this other world—mythic, eternal, symbolic—that makes his wearing of the crown a possible affront to the very god Keats would devote himself to: Apollo.

The first labor of Keats's writing of *Endymion* is apologizing to the god whose bewildering guidance he most needs:

God of the golden bow,
    And of the golden lyre,
And of the golden hair,
    And of the golden fire,
        Charioteer
        Round the patient year —
    Where, where slept thine ire,
When like a blank ideot I put on thy wreath —⁵

His hope is only that he is too lowly to be worth the god's striking him dead. Or so he fears. He also fears Jove's thunder avenging his arrogance. And then he thinks a gentle thought, a lyric thought, that Apollo's own music mutes that thunder, and creates a space of reprieve in which the poet Keats might redeem his offense. That redemptive note is struck in hearing outside the limits of his self-consciousness — mercy comes in perception:

The Pleiades were up,
    Watching the silent air;
The seeds and roots in earth
    Were swelling for summer fare;
        The ocean, its neighbour,
        Was at his old labor,
    When — who, who did dare
To tie for a moment thy plant round his brow,
        And grin and look proudly,
        And blaspheme so loudly,
    And live for that honor to stoop to thee now,
        O Delphic Apollo?⁶

Within apology, within the overwhelming need to make repair, Keats returns to sensibility, and sensibility alters ambition from fame's vaulting desire, to labor of an earthly sort: the ocean in rolling toil, the seeds in their ripening. Keats finds himself in the place of his truest crisis, the crisis *Endymion* will explore. He finds himself caught between the natural world and the godly world, witness to their inter-penetration but excluded from it. He begins his poem as a form of repair.

But for Keats the beginning never occurs in the beginning. Leaving Carisbrooke for Margate, Keats writes to Haydon not only of his doubts about Hunt's poetic nature — "There is no greater Sin after the 7 deadly than to flatter oneself into an idea of being a great Poet" — but of his deep struggle in composing a long poem: "There is an old saying, 'well begun is half done.' 'Tis a bad one. I would use instead, 'not begun at all 'till half done.' So according to that, I have not begun my Poem and consequently (a priori) can say nothing about it."[7] Keats has a sense, almost as of Dante, that the beginning occurs in the dark middle. He must labor through the poem in order to arrive at the poem, must write the woods in which he loses himself. The poem, for Keats, is not the consequence of a thinking accomplished outside its own confines, but is a world which can only be entered by the writing of the poem, a writing that doesn't clarify so much as it allows shadows to persist and grow more real, an irrational impulse to write into bewilderment, and to use the senses to discover the dark point where one discovers *I am lost*. Such work involves despair and requires courage, undermining as it is of self and self-certainty. Genius is required.

> I remember your saying that you had notions of a good Genius presiding over you. I have of late had the same thought, for things which I did half at Random are afterwards confirmed by my judgment in a dozen features of Propriety. Is it too daring to Fancy Shakespeare this Presider? When in the Isle of Wight I met with a Shakespeare in the Passage of the House at which I lodged, it comes nearer to my idea of him than any I have seen. I

was but there a Week, yet the old Woman made me take it with me though I went off in a hurry. Do you not think this is ominous of good?[8]

Dante had his Virgil to guide him and shield his eyes from the gorgon's stare; Keats has Shakespeare's likeness in his bag, to be hung on a wall and oversee the work of writing *Endymion*, drawing out from Keats those words that pull the poet's inward quality after them, worlding words, that make of the poet a dweller in his own poem. Shakespeare's genius presides over such hopes. "I never quite despair and I read Shakespeare. . . . I am very near Agreeing with Hazlitt that Shakespeare is enough for us."[9] When Keats finds himself unable to be lost in *Endymion* in the very ways that signal to him he's actually writing it, signal to him his having now truly begun, he turns away and returns to Shakespeare. Genius is a resource for the self that refuses to be located within the self. Genius is other. Keats discovers in the difficult experience of writing the long poem a poetic insight that will only come to fruition in the following years. He sees he is most himself when least himself. Keats finds in Shakespeare a sufficiency so replete it borders on overbrimming excess, a resource that cannot be exhausted by the continual mining of its pages for poetic sustenance. There is a world in Shakespeare, Keats knows, that fills up all the more for being, with each reading, further emptied. Such supply provides for Keats the very mark of his own aspiration. Writing to Benjamin Bailey, Keats explains:

> As to what you say about my being a Poet, I can return no answer but by saying that the high Idea I have of poetical fame makes me think I see it towering too high above me. At any rate I have no right to talk until Endymion is finished. It will be a test, a trial of my Powers of Imagination and chiefly of my invention. . . . I have heard Hunt say and I may be asked, why endeavour after a long

Poem? To which I should answer: do not the Lovers of Poetry like to have a little Region to wander in where they may pick and choose, and in which the images are so numerous that many are forgotten and found new in a second Reading, which may be food for a Week's stroll in the Summer?[10]

The poem has upon it but one requirement: it must be a world entire.

———

Every morning, Keats writes, we wreathe "[a] flowery band to bind us to the earth."[11] We do so because the world is the very place of experience, encounter's own ground — and experience, as Keats writes to Haydon, is the only fruit he hopes to glean from his summer spent writing *Endymion*. The world is the place of experience to which, by a flowery band, we bind ourselves; the poem is a world to which, by a line, we find ourselves bound. Keats's most immediate meaning in his letter to Haydon speaks not only to his sense of *Endymion* as an inevitable failure, but that the writing of the poem is itself the experience from which he will learn — a profit only to be found in the poems still to be written. He also hints at something harder to define, something less pragmatic, a hazy point around which revolve those curious overlaps in which poem and world intertwine without wholly coexisting, around which revolve experiences whose quality cannot be reduced simply to nerves, to event, to actuality, but whose quality hovers within experience itself as that which resists experience as its measure. Keats opens his long romance exactly within this abstract difficulty:

A thing of beauty is a joy for ever:
Its loveliness increases; it will never
Pass into nothingness; but still will keep
A bower quiet for us, and a sleep
Full of sweet dreams, and health, and quiet breathing.[12]

A "beautiful thing" and "a thing of beauty" are not identical. Where the former speaks of an object with a particular quality, that of being beautiful, the latter speaks of something derived from a beauty that seems, impossibly enough, both to be an origin, and so larger than the thing manifesting its quality, and contained within the object itself. A "thing of beauty" exists between two different senses of the world—a formative, mythical, ideal realm of which the material world is sensible realization, and simultaneously, the very matter of the material world itself, in which a thing is that which can be touched. Joy grows complicated when it is seen as a reaction to a "thing of beauty" cast in such twofold light: it is a moment's reaction precisely at the point where a moment is a version of eternity. Beauty is within the thing, but exceeds the thing—it presents itself to us as an introduction to essence. To experience essence seems to be beauty's deep promise; beauty seems to be the experience of essence. But essence also flees, and one can find that the beautiful thing, grasped in the hand, has diminished only into a thing—and its being, its essence, is elsewhere, experience's trace without experience's proof.

This faith in essence adds to every object another dimension, not only invisible, but nonexistent to an eye incapable of poetic faith. Keats's eye finds within the "thing of beauty" a mythic realm, a threshold one can learn to cross as soon as question reverts back into quest, and the work of writing the poem may be understood not merely as the attempt to make a "thing of beauty," but to enter into the "thing of beauty" the poem itself contemplates, an offering that is also a trespass. Here the work of writing and reading are one. Both are initiatory, and both seek entrance into that which seems to bar entry. The written word that contains within it the ceaseless breath by which it must again be pronounced shares the very condition of the world which it names—an object within which we find "a bower quiet," and a "sleep full of sweet dreams," and yes, "quiet breathing." The overwhelm-

ing drama Keats introduces us to in these opening lines of
Endymion, seemingly so ease-full and placid, marks out that
territory where *pneuma*, *spirit*, *soul*, interpenetrate all and
yet are nowhere to be found. Keats wants to enter into the
thing of beauty and breathe—he knows there is a "quiet
breathing" there, just there, within the thing itself—a quiet
that breathes, a pneumatic silence that is the world's breath,
and the dream one there dreams is the world's dream, from
which to awake, Keats will learn, is to find the dream true.

What is it, though, to wake within the poem? As much as
this is Keats's question, and as much as it is ours, so it is Endymion's. Endymion falls asleep in his own world only to
wake in another; every dreamer sleeps to wake in just the
same way. But Endymion's dream is more real than reality,
for he wakes into that realm that exists only because poetry
promises us it exists, that realm that requires our imaginative effort to keep it within the claim of the real. Such an
awakening occurs beneath the mind's strict ratios where
vision is loosened from sight and drags perception after it
into revelation:

> Wherein lies happiness? In that which becks
> Our ready minds to fellowship divine,
> A fellowship with essence; till we shine,
> Full alchemiz'd, and free of space . . .
> Then old songs waken from enclouded tombs;
> Old ditties sigh above their father's grave;
> Ghosts of melodious prophecyings rave
> Round every spot where trod Apollo's foot;
> Bronze clarions awake, and faintly bruit,
> Where long ago a giant battle was;
> And, from the turf, a lullaby doth pass
> In every place where infant Orpheus slept.
> Feel we these things?—that moment have we stept

Into a sort of oneness, and our state
Is like a floating spirit's. But there are
Richer entanglements, enthralments far
More self-destroying, leading, by degrees,
To the chief intensity[13]

Endymion falls asleep in his own world, only to wake in another. Beauty seems not to be a form of recognition, but a conduit, and he who enters beauty finds himself awakened at the very place where separate worlds connect. The effort of staying awake—this poetic wakefulness in the very center of sleep—occurs in a location that can never be a place, a symbolic ground in which the old songs sing themselves new, where to listen is also to be a singer, and to sing is also to be sung. The air here is spiritualized, the world's own *pneuma*, in which every spoken word continues forever in its being said, so that even to repeat a word is to participate in creation's own onward-gliding consciousness.

But to step into that "sort of oneness" comes with consequences the "consequitive mind"[14] could never guess at. The poetic mind—whose nature is reciprocal in such a way that it grasps only that which it is first grasped by—functions not by reason, but by "richer entanglements." James Land Jones, in *Adam's Dream: Mythic Consciousness in Keats and Yeats*, says: "Self-consciousness may be defined as an awareness of the separateness of the self from the world."[15] Endymion wakes—and so Keats wakes with him—into a world in which self-consciousness fails by falling into a "fellowship with essence." When the self ceases in self-knowledge, when personality falls aside as does a husk from a grain, when the wind winnows identity away with the chaff so the germ can hear the winnowing song, then we find ourselves—not as ourselves—in self-destroying enthrallments. In but a few months, when with *Endymion* all but complete, Keats will write to George and Tom that "the excellence of every Art is its intensity,"[16] he must be speaking back to what his long poem has taught him—the poem that led him, "by degrees / To the chief intensity." Such intensity is knowable only insofar as one finds something "swelling into reality" exactly where reality should be denied. Keats's language is both sexual and botanical, a ripening of potency whose only end ushers poet and poem's reader onto that strange point where, as Emerson has it, "we stand before the secret of the world, there where Being passes into Appearance, and Unity into Variety."[17] Except, Keats might add, we are not standing. There is a motion mining through the whole that urges us into the poem—the world of the poem as it swells into reality—where essence wanders through experience, fugitive and enthralling both.

Paul Celan, the great German poet whose work suffered the wound it also kept open, whose family died at Nazi hands, spoke of himself as a poet who was "stricken by and seeking reality." In the same speech, given on being awarded the Bremen prize in 1958, Celan begins by saying, "'Thinking' and 'thanking' in our language are words from one and the same source. Whoever follows out their meaning enters the semantic field of: 'recollect,' 'bear in mind,' 'remembrance,' 'devotion.'"[18]

Keats, too, is a poet in whom thinking and thanking cannot be told apart, a poet for whom memory and devotion require each other. When Endymion recalls his dream to his sister Peona, that dream in which the goddess Cynthia collects the mortal human and transports him to that heavenly bourne where his "dazzled soul / Commingling with her argent spheres"[19] loses self-definition in favor of the greater gift of immortal participation, we hear the hero trying to describe that impossible point at which consciousness ceases to be an awareness of one's separate nature. Instead, we watch as thinking grows thankful, and in that thankfulness consciousness alters dazzlingly, alters maddeningly the mind, which becomes not a crucible of self-awareness that cuts self away from the very thing of which it thinks, but makes of the mind an altar upon which the "self" of self-consciousness is sacrificed, and consciousness transforms into consummation.

To Endymion's torment, such commingling with essence immortal cannot last. Within his own dream he falls asleep: "Why did I dream that sleep o'er-power'd me / In midst of all this heaven?" When he wakes, that heaven is gone:

> Away I wander'd—all the pleasant hues
> Of heaven and earth had faded: deepest shades
> Were deepest dungeons; heaths and sunny glades
> Were full of pestilent light; our taintless rills
> Seem'd sooty, and o'er-spread with upturn'd gills
> Of dying fish; the vermeil rose had blown
> In frightful scarlet, and its thorns out-grown
> Like spiked aloe.[20]

Endymion wakes as one who finds the very veils that had been torn from his eyes covering them again. What before had been beauty's very definition has become but a sooty shadow marring a more essential beauty with appearance's meager—undeniable but needing to be denied—presence. The immortal love Endymion found himself once embraced by reduces his previous ambitions to "merest whim." His seeking after fame, "all this poor endeavour," pales in comparison to his newfound hope to be "one who keeps within his stedfast aim / A love immortal."[21] The nature of his song's burden has changed.

It is a burden that shares the quality of a dream, a burden-less burden, "more slight / Than the mere nothing that engenders them!"[22] The hardest weight to lift is the one that is weightless. Endymion (and through his hero Keats himself) finds himself in that "blessed mood" Wordsworth sings of:

In which the burthen of the mystery,
In which the heavy and the weary weight
Of all this unintelligible world
Is lighten'd: — [23]

But that burden which has no weight is made no easier to
bear by being lightened. Keats offers us a wondrous mis-
reading of Wordsworth's lines, in which burdensome mystery isn't lessened in mass, but clarified in vision. A light-
ness comes into the "unintelligible world" and brings to the
eye that which before had been denied. This light makes the
world no less unintelligible, for the eye in its most vivid seeing forsakes thought for perception — it sees the complications it enters, an act that puts reason away in the world left
behind, and seeks within the unintelligible world's tangle a
bower where sleep brings those dreams that outstrip reality.

In *Adam's Dream*, James Land Jones turns back to Mircea
Eliade's discussion of the sacred and profane as the primary
distinctions separating a mythic consciousness from a modern one. Deep inside the etymology of "poem" resides the
sense of the "made thing." A poem is a made thing. Deep inside Keats's inquiry is whether or not the "made thing" may
also be a "thing of beauty." In some sense, the drama of the
poem is the willful attention to the poem's own manifesta-
tion, the medium of our ability to attend, to dwell within,
that which the poem contains and shows forth. Outside the
poem — that place the poet occupies before the poem is
written — is a profane space, governed by time's relentlessly
mortal march. The poem establishes within itself a sacred
space, a refuge for the poet who finds himself haunted by
the lingering knowledge that at any moment, any object, any
act, holds within it the possibility of manifesting the sacred.
A sacred space, as Eliade describes it, maintains essential
differences from a profane space. Time cycles through eter-

nal returns, moving forward only so as to return to origin, and so in a more profound sense, moving not at all. Such timeless time keeps open the creative locus in which the gods created the world and continue to exist within it, available to those who make themselves available to the gods. The sacred space establishes within the very midst of the profane world's series of broken circles another center, a world-axis, around which cosmos may order itself and the music of the shattered spheres be heard again.[24]

Within that sacred center festivals don't commemorate a past event, but "re-actualize" it. *Endymion* begins in festival, though the hero, stricken by the reality of his sacred dream, cannot take part in the ceremonies or the songs. His fellow shepherds, the "young damsels" of this Arcadia, have all gathered in recognition that "[o]ur vows are wanting to our great god Pan."[25] The song they will sing marks that ground in which thinking merges into thanking, and thanking into devotion. They pray to Pan that sun and shade continue, that figs ripen, that honeycombs with honey fill, that butterflies emerge with "freckled wings," and that every potential of fruitfulness ripens into actual fruit. Pan keeps guard over those natural cycles that sustain the lives that depend upon them, and the music of his pipes encourages what it accompanies, "the force that through the green fuse drives the flower."[26] The song ensures that Pan remains in presence in the world, keeping sacred that which threatens to turn profane; the song, one could say, keeps the world in panic. Endymion, swept as he has been into the sacred world, understands, in ways that no one else around him can, that the immersion into the sacred brings with it as much terror as it does exaltation.

Keats learns the same lesson in the writing of the poem, that other transport into devoted realms. His earlier hope of being overseen by a genius, jested about with Haydon, and exemplified in the portrait of Shakespeare he hangs upon his wall, gains a new urgency within the sacred work of the poem. Retracing the history of genius in the ancient world, Giorgio Agamben writes:

> That is why the encounter with Genius is terrible. The life that maintains the tension between the personal and the impersonal, between Ego and Genius, is called poetic. But the feeling that occurs when Genius exceeds us on every side is called panic — panic at something that comes over us and is infinitely greater than what we believe ourselves able to bear.[27]

Agamben goes on, describing what a faulty attachment to genius might look like, echoing Keats's own concern, stated in the midst of writing *Endymion*, about Leigh Hunt's flattering himself into becoming a poet.

> But more laughable and fatuous than this is someone who experiences the encounter with Genius as a privilege, the Poet who strikes a pose and puts on airs or, worse, feigns humility and gives thanks for the grace received. In the face of Genius, no one is great; we are all equally small.[28]

In the most poetic of ironies, it is by undertaking Leigh Hunt's self-inflated challenge to write a four-thousand-line poem that Keats lifts off the laurel crown Hunt had placed upon his head. He takes the crown off because Keats has found in the poem itself the encounter with genius that mocks profane recognitions that vaunt the self into false relationships with those more occult powers that keep the page — the world on the page — in panic. The true laurel crown is not worn around the head, but within the mind — it is not two torn sprigs, but the mind's living bower. What Keats finds as he follows Endymion to the underworld, what he carries back in learning that love's chief intensity is one that binds immortal to mortal, fundamentally alters the ways in which he views imaginative work and the consequences upon the self of one who would spend his life writing poetry. Keats becomes capable of being overwhelmed by genius, a condition in which the ego is drowned in the "fine suddenness" by which genius introduces one to the world in all its panicked, poetic complexity — that confounding, or co-founding, of the sacred within the profane.

The senses change in such a world. The ear grows capable of knowing "[s]ilence was music from the holy spheres," and what before had been blank has become the erotic paradox of the "known Unknown."²⁹ Keats does not become a genius — to say so is to misunderstand the very meaning genius offers. Keats realizes a genius he is also realized by, encounters within himself that which is least himself, the place where *I* and *other* ease their oppositional tensions, loosen their binding definitions, and merge inexplicably into one. It is an experience thought cannot predict or comprehend, an experience of beauty — and beauty arrives, as an allegorical character of old, in her translucent, radiant gown, to banish thought back to the profane world in which logic tells you exactly where the dream ends.

Keats has learned from this experience much that will shape the molten core of his poetic thought. At the close of 1817, with *Endymion* all but complete, he writes two letters, the former opening up the insight of the latter. Writing to Benjamin Bailey, Keats says:

> I am certain of nothing but of the holiness of the Heart's affections and the truth of Imagination. What the imagination seizes as beauty must be truth — whether it existed before or not — for I have the same idea of all our Passions as of Love; they are all in their sublime, creative of essential Beauty. . . . The Imagination may be compared to Adam's dream — he woke and found it truth.³⁰

Keats sees poetry involved not in a work of representation, but as a work creative of essence. A poem opens being to

Being, but to do so, it must close off those rational corridors that make of perception mere idea. Imagination must, so to speak, nerve thought back into a grasping form; thought must learn again to ask "what is at hand" by understanding that thinking is when the hand opens. Beauty leads to that truth imagination alone can find, a truth whose eternity cannot be measured in the logician's charts or the philosopher's maxims, for it is a truth as mutable as sensation itself, no "cold pastoral," but the capillary's blush in the beautiful cheek. Keats's enthusiastic prayer for "a life of Sensations rather than of Thoughts!"[31] is *ingenious* insofar as he utters it as genius's own realization — that realm not only in which "thinking" and "thanking" share a source, but where what is genial and what is generous are one and the same. Sensation makes of the body whole a thinking thing, and the erotic becomes our dearest epistemology.

Genius also demands that the self lessen the authority of its sway, that it become impersonal exactly at the point of its greatest intimacy. It finds its startle in the moment:

> Nothing startles me beyond the Moment. The setting sun will always set me to rights, or if a Sparrow come before my Window, I take part in its existence and pick about the Gravel.[32]

This mention of becoming the sparrow he sees reads most true when read most literally. It is the gift of genius that makes one capable of being impersonal, and the impersonal acts at the necessary initiation into the existence of another. It also predicts Keats's most famous letter, written one month later:

> I had not a dispute but a disquisition with Dilke [Charles Wentworth Dilke, six years Keats's elder, and a close friend] on various subjects; several things dovetailed in my mind, and at once it struck me, what quality went to form a Man of Achievement, especially in Literature and

which Shakespeare possesses so enormously—I mean *Negative Capability*, that is when man is capable of being in uncertainties, Mysteries, doubts, without any irritable reaching after fact and reason. Coleridge, for instance, would let go by a fine isolated verisimilitude caught from the Penetralium of mystery, from being incapable of remaining content with half knowledge. This pursued through Volumes would perhaps take us no further than this, that with a great poet the sense of Beauty overcomes every other consideration, or rather obliterates all consideration.[33]

Among the lesser noticed brilliances of the passage is how *bodily* his realization is as he describes it. "Capability"—here so hauntingly in advance of his late poem "This living hand, now warm and capable"—has within its etymology being receptive in terms of being capable of holding what is put into it. The body is a capable thing, capable of holding the mind that is itself capable of holding the world imagination realizes as truth. Those who in "irritation" reach only after the incapable capacities of "fact and reason" revoke themselves from more spiritual irritations, those excitements that nerve the mind and return it to a more primary mode of consciousness, the capable center of every sense, half mythic and half erotic, whose orientation to the world it finds itself within undoes consideration's rational reign, and returns us to the genuine field, Genius's field, the Penetralium at the center of the sacred whole, whose reality cannot forsake the veils that faultily guard its mystery. Keats considered *Endymion* a failure; it was the most important failure of his poetic life.

Ascent & Descent

In the summer of 1818 Keats joined Charles Brown on a northern tour through Scotland. His younger brother Tom already showed signs of the consumption that would kill him, but Keats trusted he would fare well in the season's fair weather until his return. Keats himself felt in his constitution that which could not bear to be constantly wet; and then he travelled to where he would almost always be wet.

He came down with a sore throat that would not cease.

It is a curious ailment for the poet, a sore throat: a pain as if one must speak that keeps one from speaking. His inability to recover strikes some as a sign of the latent illness that in a few years will kill him. Keats seems to think the same. A presentiment was upon him. He calls his body "This mortal body of a thousand days"; he miscalculated by only seven weeks.[1]

The only books he took with him on his trip? A three-volume translation of Dante, small enough to fit in his pack.[2] As Keats fought through cold and damp to eventually climb the mountain Ben Nevis, he carried with him the tale of another poet descending into hell.

The poet and the hero share a mythic bond: both must step down through death in order to climb back up into life. I like to think—though it is no fact—that on top of Ben Nevis, as Keats looked down into the misty chasms, that Dante had reached hell's lowest circle where the frozen, rebel giants towered above him. I like to imagine—and it is no fact, and cannot be a fact—that Keats looked down as Dante climbed, looking up. I like to think of Dante climbing up through the depths of Keats's mind. Imagination is also a quest that descends through death only to emerge alive again into the world. But sometimes one is lost in one's own looking:

> Read me a lesson, Muse, and speak it loud
>   Upon the top of Nevis, blind in mist![3]

Keats sees to the limits of his seeing; he has no Virgil to hide his eyes from the gorgon when she comes. But his gorgon is no monster, is not Medusa. His gorgon is but the mist that clouds his vision, that makes heaven as unknowable as hell, that obscures the world as much as it obscures the self, and faces his eyes not with the eyes of a hundred snakes, not with the gorgon's fatal eyes, but with the faceless face of the fog itself, some vague nothing that looks back.

Keats and Brown also visited Fingal's Cave:

> Suppose now the Giants who rebelled against Jove had taken a whole Mass of black Columns and bound them together like bunches of matches — and then with immense Axes had made a cavern in the body of these columns; of course the roof and floor must be composed of the broken ends of the Columns. Such is Fingal's Cave except that the Sea has done the work of excavations and is continually dashing there. . . . As we approached in the boat there was a fine swell of the sea that the pillars appeared rising immediately out of the crystal. But it is impossible to describe it —[4]

The cave strikes Keats's mind so that it seems the gods still exert their presence on the world. It is a kind of poetic lesson, how place can invoke that mythic time that never passes, and reinitiate one into a first consciousness, a sacred space where those beings who created the world are still creating it. Such work has always been the poet's song. But the cave offers other lessons. It shows the beauty and horror of what it is when a ceaseless force beats forever against a limited object. So the sea beats the stone and the stone wastes away. So the throat hurts. So Keats returns home to find Tom dying, flesh thinning against bone.

1818

Failure–Genius–Self

Keats reacts to the violent criticism of *Endymion* not as any wilting flower too delicate to bear the world's buffeting, but with a resolve whose strength borders on pride. He tells one of his publishers, Hessey, that "praise or blame" can have "but a momentary effect on the man whose love of beauty in the abstract makes him a severe critic of his own Works."[1] Keats knows the failure of *Endymion* more keenly and more truly, to a deeper plummet of depth, than any critic could inflict upon him; Keats also knows that the long poem's failures are intimately entwined with its heights. He writes:

> It is as good as I had power to make it — by myself — Had I been nervous about its being a perfect piece and with that view asked advice and trembled over every page, it would not have been written; for it is not in my nature to fumble. . . . I have written independently *without Judgment*. I may write independently *and with judgment* hereafter. The Genius of Poetry must work out its own salvation in a man: It cannot be matured by law and precept, but by sensation and watchfulness in itself. That which is creative must create itself. In Endymion, I leaped headlong into the Sea, and thereby have become better acquainted with the Soundings, the quicksands, and the rocks, than if I had stayed upon the green shore, and piped a silly pipe, and took tea and comfortable advice. I was never afraid of failure; for I would sooner fail than not be among the greatest.[2]

The poet is one who from perfection learns quickly to flee. Perfection — the advice that guides one toward it, and worse, the questions that garner such advice — privileges a world-like system over a system-breaking world. In a perfect world there is only the depthless sea, the airless air. A perfect world denies the very experience by which it could be discovered. Keats forges an intuitive link between an approach to poetry so tremulous with intent that the poet's hand shakes with the force of will by which he'd write, and the resulting poem, whose beauty depends upon a Law it did not, because it could not, discover within itself. Within Keats's poetic axiom that a poem must "come . . . as naturally as the Leaves to a tree"[3] lurks a deeper ethic than "organic form" implies. He sees that a poem "must work out its own salvation in a man." The material with which the poem does this salvific work is no less than the sensations of the man in which the poem occurs. The poem seems to abstract from the nerves of the man himself that Beauty which he can only, literally, sense. The world of the poem is showered in watchfulness. The actual body becomes an un-minded thing. Then the hand doesn't write the word because it obeys the thought that commands it; no, it's the mind that fails. Seeking a way to dismantle those laws the mind would impose on what it creates, Keats realizes that the mind is no source, hardly a resource, save when it fills with that judgment that intuitively guides the eyes to where they should look, and asks secretly, unobtrusively, for the hand to open and grasp what must be grasped. There abstraction begins, and the poet is as an alembic in which a distillation occurs that he cannot wholly control, a mystic vessel, not creative in itself, but in whose crucible that which is creative "must create itself."

———

Two weeks later, Keats writes one of his most famous letters:

> As to the poetical Character itself (I mean that sort of which, if I am anything, I am a Member; that sort distinguished from the wordsworthian or egotistical sublime, which is a thing per se and stands alone), it is not itself—

it has no self—it is everything and nothing—It has no
character. . . . What shocks the virtuous philosopher, de-
lights the camelion Poet. . . . A Poet is the most unpoetical of anything in existence because he has no Identity;
he is continually in for and filling some other Body.[4]

This sense of the poetic self as no self at all, this belief that a
certain kind of poet retreats from the ego's formative fact as
quickly as dew departs from the sun, is the abstracted judgment Keats gains from plummeting into the dangers of *Endymion*'s failure. That world of Sea and quicksands, of grassy
bowers and Caves of Despondence, depends on an imagined landscape not wholly distilled from the actual world.
The epic landscape encountered in Scotland, those chasms
filled with mists, poured into Keats through those very ruptures the failure of *Endymion* opened in him, the failure *Endymion* opened him to. Failure deepened Keats's receptive
capacity. Keats not only "was never afraid of failure," but it
is through his very willingness to fail that he will become, if
he is to become, one "among the greatest."

Well, *willingness* might be the wrong word. For it is precisely in the failure of the will that Keats finds his astonishing gift. Will is a curious labyrinth, wandering through
the self only to find the self in the maze's middle, not mon-
strous, but plotting. Failure offers a gift seen most readily in
the will's sudden incapacity, a dismantling that pulls apart
other forms of pride, each thought to be fundamental, but
the fundaments are in ruin: mind's reason, faith's light,
ethic's right, and self's self-same sanctity.

Keats discovers in himself the miracle that he is not himself. The "Genius of Poetry" that worked out its own salvation within Keats—regardless or disregarding of Keats's
own salvation—is also a Genius of Failure. Genius is when
the self suffers a breakage from one into many and "I" becomes anonymous, choral, and the mind not a pot, but
a putty. Genius breaks the self to open the self, makes of

the senses portals through which the world waterfalls into that fragmented self who cannot contain what fills it. If the Genius of Poetry teaches us to say "I," it teaches us to say "I" as another. One could hazard to say that genius is the failure of the self to remain a self.

Indolence–Ambition–Imagination

The erotic mind is apprentice to contrary educations: pursuit and passivity. In some under-grove of ardor's epistemology, Apollo forever chases Daphne; in some under-arbor, a poet falls asleep to wake and find a laurel crown circling his head, a remnant vision in his eye. But in Keats's poetry, it is the remnant that is excessive:

> In Poetry I have a few Axioms, and you will see how far I am from their Centre. First, I think Poetry should surprise by a fine excess and not by Singularity; it should strike the Reader as a wording of his own highest thoughts, and appear almost a Remembrance.[5]

Keats knows those axioms that might be the dense points of his poetic discovery cannot become the axis of his poetic practice without deadening the vagrancy his art depends on. Keats is astray.

Keats is astray, but his wandering occurs in a spectrum, a pendulum motion swinging toward an ambition in which he thinks he "shall be among the English Poets after my death,"[6] to an indolence "abominably idle."[7] Both extremes contain their dangers, and Keats is keenly aware of them. That drive to write a great poem, that *designed* ambition, sacrifices the ambiguities of discovery for the grandeur of intent. It is a poetry Keats abhors, even as his ambitions propel him toward uncomfortable sympathy with the desire to be great.

> We hate poetry that has a palpable design upon us — and if we do not agree, seems to put its hands in its breeches pocket. Poetry should be great and unobtrusive, a thing which enters into one's soul and does not startle it or amaze it with itself but with its subject.[8]

Keats sees that a poem is not an argument to convince, but an evidence of conviction. The poem that in its singularity forces the reader to admit of its greatness betrays those uncertain gifts genuine poetry offers—the half-lit realm in which thought arrives as experience, and an idea is a sensational value. Concepts grow nervous as "a sensitive leaf on the hot hand of thought."[9] That leaf is a flower's petal and an ash's leaf; it is also the page of a poem.

Recognition comes with a shock. Keats has one such shock at Hunt's, when he is told the lock of hair he is holding comes from the head of Milton.

> For many years my offerings must be hush'd.
>   When I do speak, I'll think upon this hour,
> Because I feel my forehead hot and flush'd—
>   Even at the simplest vassal of thy power;
>   A lock of thy bright hair—
>   Sudden it came,
> And I was startled, when I caught thy name
>   Coupled so unaware;
> Yet at the moment, temperate was my blood—
> Methought I had beheld it from the Flood.[10]

That lock of Milton's hair acts as a strange catalyst to Keats's poetic mind. It tempers the fever of his intent; it deepens his imagination's erotic flush. Keats experiences a radical, because bodily, form of synecdoche. The lock of hair not only stands in for Milton himself (this lesser substitution would only feed the ego of the poet who would dearly wish to be Milton's equal), but represents all that Milton thought, as if in growing out of the head it also grew out of the mind, and bore in its strands some residue of that lost paradise Milton in his blindness saw with such glaring, dark brilliance. Keats holds in his hand a relict, one that makes palpable the moment in which the pre-Edenic world became the post-Edenic, a moment in which desire and knowledge so intertwined that the consequence was no less than the loss of paradise, the fall into a language that must want in order to know. That fall links desire to knowledge in ways that deeply complicate both, a knot intrinsicate, where facts grow amorous as their definitions fail. This same fall also alters our sense of Beauty, that ever-tightening, ever-loosening concatenation of wanting and knowing. Keats feels it keenly. So keenly he comes to a sense of art in which he grows aware of those "innumerable compositions and decompositions which take place between the intellect and its thousand materials before it arrives at that trembling delicate and snail-horn perception of Beauty."[11] Keats is asking a question about the eye. Or, it may be more accurate to say, his eye is asking a question of Keats. How does the poet see? The answer is that a poet sees by letting his eye reach into the beauty it perceives.

But how to teach the eye not to take in light, but to reach into it? How to reverse the eye's own order, altering it from that which only receives, to that which, hand-like, must grasp toward what it would see?

One answer is to become lazy.

One answer is to laze in the field's long grasses until one becomes field-like — until one becomes an aspect of the field.

Keats feels, at the very onset of the year, that something in him has altered: "I think a little change has taken place in my intellect lately. I cannot bear to be uninterested or un-employed, I, who for so long a time had been addicted to passiveness."[12] This isn't to say that Keats has broken his ad-diction with a dose of industry; it means that his addiction itself has suffered a change, has nurtured itself in its own need, and has inverted its nature from a state that allows the world to go by with no concern, to a form of work itself, a kind of labor — I might say, a *kind* labor — that attends to the world by the world's own means. Keats's indolence be-comes mimetic; or, to put it in a language dearer to Keats's heart, his indolence becomes that deep virtue that allows him not only to withstand the "uncertainties, Mysteries, doubts" that negative capability demands he withstand; indolence permits him to *stand within* those unstable quiddities that mark the tenor of his genius.

This "diligent Indolence!"[13] sifts down, as pollen sifts down from a pine, into every nuance of Keats's poetic epistemology. It immediately affects his notion of Imagination.

> It has been an old Comparison for our urging on—the Bee hive—however, it seems to me that we should rather be the flower than the Bee, for it is a false notion that more is gained by receiving than giving. No, the receiver and the giver are equal in their benefits. The flower, I doubt not, receives a fair guerdon from the Bee. Its leaves blush deeper in the next spring, and who shall say between Man and Woman which is the most delighted? Now it is more noble to sit like Jove than to fly like Mercury. Let us not therefore go hurrying about and collecting honey-bee like, buzzing here and there impatiently from a knowledge of what is to be arrived at; but let us open our leaves like a flower and be passive and receptive, budding patiently under the eye of Apollo and taking hints from every noble insect that favors us with a visit.[14]

Keats gives us no less than a parable of the Imagination in which Indolence serves as the primary poetic discovery. Here, the natural and the erotic revel one in another, an inversion of the field that also inverts human sexual relations, in which pleasure and passivity, pleasure *in* passivity, is the man's fair reward as much as it is the woman's. That bee-like industry of gathering the field into the hive borders upon a poetic effort Keats holds in ever-greater doubt, a poetry of "palpable design" that aims at an end it knows in advance: fame's honey, a poetry that teases with "grandeur and merit." Keats suggests that when Imagination becomes an activity, an intent, it sentences itself to being merely a productive mode whose guaranteed result sacrifices the poem to a known, knowable end, that more indolent dwelling in the field might undermine entirely. But to become like the field, the flower-full field, to become the flower itself, trusts to a patience that insists only that what arrives does so as a gift, unscripted, unplanned, open to those chance encounters whose end is no more, no less, than the furthering of the field entire.

How to teach the eye, like the snail's horn, to reach into vision? Learn that a flower is an eye on a stalk; then open your eye. Then the eye is sustaining; so is every sense, leaves all unfolded:

> Sap will be given us for Meat and dew for drink. I was led into these thoughts, my dear Reynolds, by the beauty of the morning operating on a sense of Idleness. I have not read any books. The Morning said I was right. I had no Idea but of the Morning, and the Thrush said I was right, seeming to say:
> "O thou whose face hath felt the Winter's wind,
> Whose eye has seen the Snow clouds hung in Mist . . .
> O thou whose only book has been the light
> Of supreme darkness which thou feddest on
> Night after night . . .
> O fret not after knowledge—I have none
> And yet my song comes native with the warmth.
> O fret not after knowledge—I have none
> And yet the Evening listens."[15]

The thrush teaches John Keats the nature of his song. He learns from it that whatever knowledge will be his, it is a knowledge that must manna-like come. And if there is none, if no knowledge is gained, knowledge is anyway only an accident of song, and there is still the song, a song with no intent, just a singing, to whose native tune the whole world tends.

Knowledge–Thought–Confusion

Knowledge vexes Keats's poetic, ceasing to be reason's certain end, and becoming instead the threshing ground in which thought and consideration, sensation and beauty, beat one against another, chaff carried away by the inspiring wind, the known seeds carried away by those reapers who know in advance what is good from what is bad, and the poet left to glean the confused remnants. That threshing ground is the poet's mind:

> When I have fears that I may cease to be
>   Before my pen has glean'd my teeming brain,
> Before high piled books, in charactry,
>   Hold like rich garners the full ripen'd grain . . .[16]

Poetic agriculture is a mortal work. In 1818, as Keats falls ever deeper into a sense of his life's not distant limits, he comes to see the work of the "teeming brain" as one that keeps store for an immortal life which feeds, but cannot save, the mortal one. The mind is a threshing ground; the pen, a gleaner's tool; the book, a granary. Keats's organic sense of the poem—"if Poetry comes not as naturally as the Leaves to a tree it had better not come at all"[17]—presupposes poetic activity as one that mimics agricultural rhythms, agricultural rites. Poetry unfolds a leaf in the mind, but that leaf isn't the poem, merely its evidence. The poem results from another process: that gleaning by pen of the mind that finds in scattered seeds a poetic source. Such searching is not a rational activity. Knowledge is needed, but knowing isn't knowledge's end. Knowledge may be no more than the pen that does the gleaning: the sensitive tool.

Deep within the notion of the poem's organic life resides a sense of the mind that is not only cyclical in the agricultural sense (and so, likewise, cyclical in a mythic sense, in which each year is a return to origin, and not an addition to time), but reminiscent of a mind itself in motion, or—it may be truer to say—of a motion in the mind. "We talk of the immense number of Books, the Volumes ranged thousands by thousands, but perhaps more goes through the human intelligence in 12 days than ever was written."[18] Hidden within Keats's earlier prayer for a "life of Sensations" rather than a life of thought lurks an unfolding realization that knowledge must come to exist in the mind as a nervous system, and not as rationality's grid. Knowledge becomes a kind of latticework upon which stray seeds might catch and grow.

Knowledge seems to function—as does a lattice—by a principle of contradiction. But contradiction need not be as logical in our imagining it as a lattice suggests:

Now it appears to me that almost any Man may like the Spider spin from his own inwards his own airy Citadel. The points of leaves and twigs on which the Spider begins her work are few and she fills the Air with a beautiful circuiting. Man should be content with as few points to tip with the fine Webb of his Soul and weave a tapestry empyrean, full of Symbols for his spiritual eye, of softness for his spiritual touch, of space for his wandering, of distinctness for his Luxury. But the Minds of Mortals are so different and bent on such diverse Journeys that it may at first appear impossible for any common taste and fellowship to exist between two or three under these suppositions. It is, however, quite the contrary. Minds would leave each other in contrary directions, traverse each other in Numberless points, and at last greet each other at the Journey's end.[19]

Beyond the beauty of imagining human intellectual endeavor as countless spider webs attached one to another rather than a library housing an "immense number of Books," we find an image that is also a theory of the poetic mind. That mind is both threshold and place of capture. It seems — spider-like — to attach itself to those leaves on those trees sprung up in the brain and leaps into that nothing it also hopes to cross. Knowledge is a web spanning that chaotic space between poetic realities, catching what motes or mites it can.

But Keats — wondrously, typically — settles into no single vision of what knowledge might be. He consistently reconceptualizes epistemological models, each related to the other, but each altering, confounding, complicating, what a poetic theory of knowledge might be.

Well, I compare human life to a large Mansion of Many Apartments, two of which I can only describe, the doors of the rest being as yet shut upon me. The first we step into we call the infant or thoughtless Chamber, in which we remain as long as we do not think. We remain there a long while, and notwithstanding the doors of the second Chamber remain wide open, showing a bright appearance, we care not to hasten to it, but are at length imperceptibly impelled by the awakening of the thinking principle within us. We no sooner get into the second Chamber, which I shall call the Chamber of Maiden-Thought, than we become intoxicated with the light and the atmosphere, we see nothing but pleasant wonders and think of delaying there forever in delight. However, among the effects this breathing is father of is that tremendous one of sharpening one's vision into the heart and nature of Man, of convincing one's nerves that the World is full of Misery and Heartbreak, Pain, Sickness and oppression, whereby This Chamber of Maiden Thought becomes gradually darken'd and at the same time on all sides of it many doors are set open, but all dark, all leading to dark passages. We see not the balance of good and evil. We are in a Mist. *We* are now in that state. We feel the "burden of the Mystery."[20]

Thinking works against knowledge. To begin to think is to step inside a motion that refuses to let us dwell in those bright comforts we most desire to reside in. Keats suspects that in his mind, every twelve days, some sum of intellectual experience courses through him that is larger than all the books ever written contain. "To know" isn't to contain it. "To think" isn't to fill up the garner. To think is to find a way to enter into the motion coursing through the mind, to not fight against it, to be moved within it. The work there to be done is strange and contrary. It is to be moved and not moved. It requires of the self a capacity to undo the self's stiff boundary into something more porous, more pliant, something through which thinking's whole motion can course without being dammed (lest the stagnant water grow fetid, and the eyes cloud with a poisoned vapor), a thousand-threaded web, a skein of mingled yarn, or the retina of the eye, whose etymology is a "net." The poet's mind isn't seeking a thought that leads to a knowledge that can be used. Knowledge is something else, something unexpected, "even like a kind of Pleasure Thermometer."[21] Knowledge in Keats's poetic epistemology attunes us exactly to what cannot be made of use, that place where sensation flees from recognition to privilege a realization that is never still, never static. Here, imagination imbues knowledge with an erotic urgency, magnetic in its pull, and knowledge grows fanciful and its fancy roams. It teaches us, as it taught Keats, that "Pleasure never is at home."[22] It flees from us as does a nightingale into the night's gloom. Knowledge requires thinking, and thinking repels us from "what we know." Keats accomplishes a profound reversal of our own epistemological assumptions. Thinking pushes us toward passages dark to our eyes, and the door to every passage is open. Thinking, for Keats, brings us to mystery; it does not dispel it. Thinking allows our eyes to see what our eyes cannot see, a darker darkness by which we sense, we do not know, that a door is open—and thinking, whether we want to or not, forces us to step through a door into what we do not know.

It is for such dark reasons—not for rationality's categories of closable rooms—that the poet is in such need of knowledge. Keats feels this is true, for *feeling* is now synonymous, symptomatic, of *knowing*. He feels knowingly, knows feelingly. Knowledge grows nervous, as it must, when he must rely on what he knows in order to enter those dark passages where knowledge has no power to cast light and expel shadow, but has power only to enter into what seems like nothingness, and offer back to the poet "[t]he feel of not to feel it."[23] How else to know one is in abyss?

> An extensive knowledge is needful to thinking people; it takes away the heat and fever and helps, by widening speculation, to ease the Burden of the Mystery. . . . The difference of high Sensations with and without knowledge appears to me this: in the latter case we are falling continually ten thousand fathoms deep and being blown up again without wings and with all the horror of a bare-shouldered Creature. In the former case, our shoulders are fledged, and we go thro' the same air and space without fear.[24]

Knowledge gives odd wings. I want to say that woven across every threshold to those dark passages is a spider's web. To walk through the threshold is to step through that web. The poet steps into darkness just as he falls into chasm; both describe the same motion, negative capability's leap. The thin strands in their silken thousands trail behind the poet, wing-like, confusing apprehension into all its meanings — fear, grasping, understanding — and this knowing web gathers into it that which slows the poet's terrible fall, as a spider, too, falls slower through the air for the web, like a parachute, above it. Or "wing-like" is a fearful phrase, and the webs are wings exactly, allowing the poet to feel what he falls through, and by feeling it, use the speed of his own fathomless drop to navigate fearlessly within thinking's abysmal plunge. Knowing does not end our confusion; it gives it to us. Knowing lets confusion become our half-lit home.

Abstraction–Wonder–Witness

Keats walked to Scotland with a purpose in mind: "I shall learn poetry here and shall henceforth write, more than ever, for the abstract endeavour of being able to add a mite to that mass of beauty which is harvested from these grand materials, by the finest spirits, and put into etherial existence for the delight of one's fellows."[25] Now, preparing to climb Ben Nevis, Keats writes a letter to Bailey in which, almost as an aside, he mentions the sense of his own death upon him. "I intend to pass a whole year with George if I live to the completion of the three next."[26] He hopes to visit his brother and sister-in-law, who are sailing over to America even as he writes this letter, if he lives long enough to do so. He seems to doubt he will. His sore throat comes to him almost as an abstract prophecy, warning him his days are dwindling.

A few weeks later, at the beginning of August, Keats and Brown climb Ben Nevis. It is on this mountain, with his sore throat in its slow burning, that Keats comes closest to that encounter with those "grand materials" whose abstraction he hopes will lend to his poems that portion of Beauty's mass he seeks. The higher he climbs, the more fascinated he is by the chasms that plummet down.

> Talking of chasms, they are the finest wonder of the whole. They appear great rents in the very heart of the mountain, though they are not, being at the side of it, but other huge crags arising round it give the appearance to Nevis of a shattered heart or Core in itself. These Chasms are 1500 feet in depth and are the most tremendous places I have ever seen; they turn one giddy if you

choose to give way to it. We tumbled in large stones and set the echoes at work in fine style. Sometimes these chasms are tolerably clear, sometimes there is a misty cloud which seems to steam up, and sometimes they are entirely smothered with clouds.[27]

These chasms act upon Keats's imagination, drawing it down into the wonder of a world made most real by the echoing sound of the rocks rising back out from the unfathomable depths into which he cast them. Those sounds come to him as if from the under-groves of the underworld, clear in his ear despite the mist that clouds his vision. Those mists, their obscuring veils, re-echo in Keats's mind as, sitting on the mountain's peak, he composes a memorial sonnet:

> I look into the chasms, and a shroud
>   Vaprous doth hide them; just so much I wist
> Mankind do know of hell: I look o'erhead,
>   And there is sullen mist; even so much
> Mankind can tell of heaven: mist is spread
>   Before the earth beneath me; even such,
> Even so vague is man's sight of himself.
>   Here are the craggy stones beneath my feet;
> Thus much I know, that, a poor witless elf,
> I tread on them; that all my eye doth meet
>   Is mist and crag—not only on this height,
> But in the world of thought and mental might.[28]

As thrilled as he is by wonder at the landscape with its epical plunges, his imagination falters where knowing begins. The sonnet marks a curious failure: a failure of abstraction. Keats uses the word in an oddly specific, nearly archaic way—one likely pulled from his medical education, still so vulnerable to a language inherited from centuries before (and practices to match the diction). Abstraction in that context signified the distillation of a substance into a more ideal or essential form. Keats means it in just such a way. He seeks to find a method by which the imagination distills the brute fact of the world into an essential Beauty, an ideal realm made possible by the material of this world, but etherealized so that the seed of its existence requires the mind's heat to germinate and bloom. A "shroud vaprous" obstructs his vision into ideal realms, into heaven and into hell, and worse, into his sight of himself. That mist is deadly. That is, the mist is a shroud, and as such, it cloaks the abstract world's essence in the knowledge that death occurs, is occurring; even as one lives, death's vaporous shroud clouds what one strives to see. Keats has a mist in his throat, a cloudy foreknowledge, not an abstract pain, but a pain that counters abstraction.

Down from the mountain, Keats finds his sore throat so severe that he cuts his trip short. He returns to London to find his youngest brother Tom no longer recuperating from illness, but worsening. Tom is dying. It is no abstraction. He is dying and Keats knows it. He is dying from the very ailment that will kill Keats himself, and Keats knows it. Keats comes home and steps straight into the cloud.

———————

Keats cares for Tom as Tom worsens, but this nursing takes a toll. Writing to Dilke, he confesses his difficulty:

> I wish I could say Tom was any better. His identity presses upon me so all day that I am obliged to go out, and although I intended to have some time to study alone, I am obliged to write, and plunge into abstract images to ease myself of his countenance, his voice and feebleness—so that I live now in a continual fever.[29]

The very marker of Keats's poetic nature, his lack of identical character that allows the unique existence of others to press upon him as a seal presses upon hot wax, causes now a crisis that cannot result in poetry. Keats becomes Tom as he cares for Tom, a fever that deranges the senses—deranges them not toward that rearrangement of which wonder partially consists, deranges them not into the abstracted ideal, but deranges them as a mist deranges vision. Abstraction is denied by the knowledge of death. Keats doesn't witness this knowledge; it presses upon him so that witness itself cannot be borne.

Tom's countenance, and the voice that feebly speaks through his brother's face, torments Keats — a torment that feels "like a crime" to him. The profundity of his difficulty not only arises through his love for his brother as he watches him waste away, but lurks darkly within Keats's poetic nature. Keats is, or would be, a witness to abstract realms. Keats sees in his poems as he can because the existence of others presses into him — he is, as a poet, an abstraction of those he encounters and, in encountering, becomes. But Tom presses into him in ways that deny his imaginative pliancy, his abstract fluidity. Tom is as one who has "seen the Gorgon." He is one who is dead without having died, one who lives without being alive. This condition mimics Keats's poetic essence even as it denies the existence of the same. Keats's profound power as a poet resides in his ability to see from within an abstracted plane that, similar to his brother's condition, exists without existing, a placeless place, a realm in between subjectivity and de-subjectification.[30] There the self is caught within un-selfing's ongoing reversal, being and nonbeing, world and chaos, from which point of crisis Keats pays witness to two worlds always falling away one from another, the actual world and the abstract world. It's his presence, not as man, not as identity or personality, but as poet, that insists these oppositions depend on one another. Such witness refuses the tendency of the abstract to part from the actual, refuses the separation of the imaginary and the real.

But Tom's face, his feeble voice, challenge his brother — not his love, but his art. A day after he confesses his difficulty to Dilke, he writes to Reynolds that "I have relapsed into those abstractions which are my only life."[31] The language here is telling. He speaks as one who returns to illness or addiction. It is a turn that turns away from Tom—not the brother turning away, but the poet, who in seeing Tom also sees as Tom sees, who in being near Tom becomes him, for then the poet too has stared into the gorgon's eyes, and the knowing that then occurs becomes a "vaporous shroud" obscuring heaven and hell alike, clouding even one's seeing within oneself, and that knowledge is nothing more than the fact that *I am dying.*

Magnet–Pursuit–Gap

Somewhere in our human depths, in the iron diffuse in the blood, or in the heart's hysterical wandering, is a magnet called desire. One who desires doesn't step toward what is wanted, but is pulled toward it. Eros's string is an invisible cord that quickens the heart as it impels the body. In October, Keats is introduced to a cousin of the Reynolds sisters, a woman from East India. Keats describes her:

> When she comes into a room she makes an impression the same as the Beauty of a Leopardess. . . . I am at such times too much occupied in admiring to be awkward or on a tremble. I forget myself entirely because I live in her. You will think I am in love with her, so before I go any further I will tell you I am not. She kept me awake one Night as a tune of Mozart's might do. . . . I don't cry to take the moon home with me in my Pocket, nor do I fret to leave her behind me. . . . She walks across a room in such a manner that a Man is drawn towards her with a magnetic Power.[32]

As much as Beauty had been for Keats "a fellowship with essence,"[33] that sense of essence has become one that cannot exclude mysterious transformations, intense and isolated impressions, that name more truly for misnaming entirely. Essence isn't identity, but invitation. The woman is a Leopardess, and Keats, in seeing her not as *beautiful* but as Beauty, becomes himself a Leopardess. He recounts his sudden passion in ways that parallel to a remarkable degree his letter to Woodhouse describing the poet as "the most unpoetical of anything in existence because he has no Identity." Keats sees and becomes: "I forget myself entirely because I live in her." His attraction speaks to the erotic on multiple levels. Simply enough, there is the sexual — but the sexual here has poetic depths, and privileges necessary forms of incompletion over any drive toward satisfaction. This is desire that grows desirous, empties the wanting self of the self so only wanting remains, destabilizes what or who it is that says "I" so only the saying remains, and when that self returns, when I can say "I" again and mean just myself, desire has left its trace, a music so deeply felt it is almost a scent, Mozart's tune in the night. Desire might by another name be called magnetism, and Beauty be called magnet. Keats is pulled into the essence of the being into which he disappears, impelled across that gap that should keep apart the fact of one existence from the definite sanctity of another, a ruptured gap, an erotic dissolution.

Poetry introduces us to abyss in all its varieties, and Keats has become a traveler not only "in the realms of gold,"[34] but a wanderer through absence, too. Imagination leaps ahead of what the eye can see, and drags vision after it, bringing the dark world into view. The poet doesn't have a vision, he follows vision. Sometimes it shows him what he would not see:

> . . . Things cannot to the will
> Be settled, but they tease us out of thought.
> Or is it that imagination brought
> Beyond its proper bound, yet still confined, —
> Lost in a sort of purgatory blind,
> Cannot refer to any standard law
> Of either earth or heaven? — It is a flaw
> In happiness to see beyond our bourn —
> It forces us in summer skies to mourn:
> It spoils the singing of the nightingale.[35]

"Flaw" here bears in it one of its oldest senses: a spot where turf is cut out. The "flaw in happiness" speaks not simply of defect, but of an opening, as if cut into the earth, and through which imagination guides us into "a sort of purgatory blind." We fall through a gap in happiness and end up confined in a world whose laws we cannot know, and those senses that might grope their way to a recognizable world are, when we "see beyond our bourn," annulled, disabled. The eye sees only that it cannot see, Keats's half-light becomes no light at all, and the ear is also blind, and deaf to the nightingale's song.

Imagination is dangerous when it precedes experience, but the poet, Keats knows, must risk such danger. The importance of the step into imagined realms isn't that it's voluntary. To intend confusion is feckless. The importance is that the step is involuntary. One follows what cannot *not* be followed. It feels like fate, and fate is, in part, where self-knowledge is revealed as fiction, and some other capacity of the self—the self that cannot know itself because it is no self—emerges.

> It is an awful mission,
> A terrible division,
> And leaves a gulf austere
> To be fill'd with worldly fear.[36]

But that "terrible division," that "gulf austere," is not only a gap that fills with "worldly fear"; it also fills with world; it also fills with worlds.

Endymion had, in part, opened in Keats just such a gap—a gap Endymion himself experiences in the poem—that fills alternately with world and with despair. Keats thinks the poem a failure, but assures his publisher Taylor that "when I wrote it, it was regular stepping of the Imagination towards a Truth."[37] The imagination, for Keats, has as its highest aspiration a stepping toward truth that realizes truth, not as a concept or idea, but as "Adam's dream"; it realizes to make real. As much as imagination risks putting one in a world that can only be filled by insensate fears, it also promises the entrance into the reality of the world that can be real in no other way. This stepping through a flaw in happiness into reality as an ongoing process is a deeply erotic activity, for it can only occur through desire, and desire's self-dismissal.

> As Tradesmen say, everything is worth what it will fetch, so probably every mental pursuit takes its reality and its worth from the ardour of the pursuer—being in itself a nothing. Ethereal things may at least be thus real, divided under three heads: Things real, things semi-real, and no things. Things real—such as existences of Sun, Moon and Stars and passages of Shakespeare—Things semi-real, such as Love, the Clouds, etc., which require a greeting of the Spirit to make them wholly exist, and Nothings, which are made Great and dignified by an ardent pursuit, which by the by stamps the burgundy mark on the bottles of our Minds . . .[38]

Ardor is arduous: passion alone provides enthusiasm enough to pass over those chasms imagination opens, chasms which must be crossed to keep real those "Nothings" upon which existence might secretly depend. This work is not a wandering, not a journey; it is an ardent, erotic pursuit. It proceeds by abandonment.

> What a happy thing it would be if we could settle our thoughts . . . that is, to build a sort of mental Cottage of feelings quiet and pleasant, to have a sort of Philosophical Back Garden and cheerful holiday-keeping front one. But Alas! this can never be, for as the material Cottager knows there are such places as [F]rance and Italy and the Andes and the Burning Mountains, so the spiritual Cottager has knowledge of the terra semi-incognita of things unearthly and cannot for his Life keep in the check rein—Or I should stop here quiet and comfortable in my theory of Nettles. You will see, however, I am obliged to run wild, being attracted by the Loadstone Concatenation.[39]

Keats feels a magnetic pull—a "Loadstone Concatenation"—tugging him helplessly, without will, without fore-
thought's design, into the wildness in which a world is discovered. Or, worlds are discovered, plural. For every link in
the chain, every magnetic link, makes solid for a moment
the nothing it encircles, and right there, the poet does his
work—not to dwell, but to enter into the next wilderness,
unseen but beckoning, pulling the poet's magnetic life into
the larger magnet of its own.

Each link is a thought, and each thought a sensation.
"It is an old maxim of mine and of course well known
that every point of thought is the centre of an intellectual
world."[40] Through the very center of each intellectual world
penetrates the peripheral link of the subsequent one. Keats
doesn't know it; he feels it. His imagination—wholly eroti-
cized—reveals it: "I feel more and more every day, as my
imagination strengthens, that I do not live in this world
alone but in a thousand worlds."[41] Each one of those worlds
is a single magnetic link in the Loadstone Concatenation.
His imagination strengthens by becoming more sensitive to
those magnetic links which—like an iron filing to the pulling stone—draw him into the larger being of a "thousand
worlds." For the poet, such realities are not to be denied.

Of Thrushes & Sparrows (A Palimpsest, 1817–1820)

So easy to forget how accuracy is a form of strangeness. In the early depths of his poetic life, Keats is most himself when least himself—less a thought, more a sensation. Where thought seeks truth beyond fact, sensation denies the same. Sensation is the border guard that laughs as trespass occurs. Self leaves self and enters the world, imagination's travail. World enters self and establishes a world, imagination's dwelling. Such a mind undermines its own working by seeking that "fine suddenness" that shocks it out of its deliberate orbit. The mind tumbles down to the fingers as those seek to apprehend what it is at hand, fact as the found thing, mere moment: the startling moment when the sun sets, "or if a Sparrow come before my Window, I take part in its existence and pick about the Gravel."[1] One way to draw an accurate portrait of Keats would be to drop some crumbs on the windowsill and wait for the sparrows to come.

No one likes to think about how strenuous it is to maintain one's own face so it is recognizable to oneself. It is a kind of ambition, not to be known so much as to be knowable. We do this for ourselves as much as we do so for others. For all Keats's singularity of person, for all the solidifying drive of his over-vaulting ambition, he could also take that ambition off as a masquerader might take off his mask. Indolence allows the world access to oneself in ways ambition cannot. Then one puts away the thought of one's own giftedness, and begins a different sort of labor—a labor that looks almost like laziness, and allows the gift of the world to less warily approach. It is the labor of one who would live on manna. "Sap will be given us for Meat and dew for drink. . . . The Morning said I was right . . . and the Thrush said I was right . . ."[2]

Later, the happiness whose nature it is to fly from the confines of the self, as a fledgling might fly from the nest, becomes happiness with a threat inside it.

> It is a flaw
> In happiness to see beyond our bourn —
> It forces us in summer skies to mourn:
> It spoils the singing of the nightingale.[3]

Sometimes a great accuracy is a greater inaccuracy. What is the form of such a flaw? The song ruined in the bird's very throat? Or something in the ear of he who listens, some error in the ear which so amazes the song that it ceases to be song?

Here's Charles Brown's account of Keats composing "Ode to a Nightingale":

> In the spring of 1819 a nightingale had built her nest near my house. Keats felt a tranquil and continual joy in her song; and one morning he took his chair from the breakfast-table to the grass-plot under a plum-tree, where he sat for two or three hours. When he came into the house, I perceived he had some scraps of paper in his hand, and these he was quietly thrusting behind the books. On inquiry, I found those scraps, four or five in number, contained his poetic feeling on the song of our nightingale. The writing was not well legible; and it was difficult to arrange the stanzas on so many scraps. With his assistance I succeeded, and this was his *Ode to a Nightingale*, a poem which has been the delight of every one.[4]

We cannot know how the song arrived to Keats, complete and in order, or in confounded fragments. We cannot know the happiness within which the poem was composed. "Scrap" likely derives its meaning onomatopoetically: the sound of a surface being scraped. As the nightingale sang, Keats scratched on scraps his companion song. Hiding the scraps behind the books he offers us a glimpse, through his friend's recollection, of how we might need to read his Ode. We must find the snatches of song hidden among the order of others' words, and we must assemble ourselves the scraps into their melodious order. That chance of making a mistake is the very accuracy of the song.

Fanny Brawne's seal, which closed the envelopes of the letters she sent Keats, was a sparrow perched upon a broken lyre. Keats would often sleep with her letters beneath his pillow, and when once he awoke to find the seal disappeared, sparrow and song both flown, he felt a dark omen.

In his late letters to Fanny, when Keats knew he was dying, when the letters filled themselves with the angry fever of a fate he could not reconcile himself to, he often hears a thrush singing even as he writes. "Do you hear the Thrush singing over the field?"[5] If she does, the song itself denies the distance separating them; the song itself brings them together.

Keats also confounds himself with the bird. "I will not sing in a cage—,"[6] he writes. He writes, "Do not I see a heart naturally furnish'd with wings imprison itself with me?"[7]

The nightingale is a thrush whose song has sung unchanged from ancient days to now, a deathless song, a song that sings through death. The nightingale of the ode is immortal because it lives within its song; its song does not live within it. Keats hopes to be among the immortals when he dies. He fears he has left "no immortal work behind me."[8] Perhaps one cannot see what one is within — the song one lives within, as if the thrush could to itself be deaf, and in singing not know it sings. The only comfort, in the end, is that other song that let him look away from the page. "There's the thrush again. I can't afford it. He'll run me up a pretty Bill for Music. . . . I shall always remember it. . . . I could build an Altar to you for it."[9] The only altar is the next blank page.

1819

Of the Odes: A Speculative Context

Keats composed the six odes for which he is most famous
in only six months, March to September. On either side of
their composition stand the ruins of two abandoned epics:
Hyperion and *The Fall of Hyperion*. Those epic efforts—the
former Miltonic in feel, the latter invested with Dante's lyric
"I"—take as their concern the result of a great battle between the old gods, when the Titans fell to the strength and
beauty of the Olympians. The drama of the two poems occurs a fathom deeper than the grand action of immortals at
war; Keats finds himself concerned with a moment in which
one order of power subsides to another power (concerned
enough that he returns to the same material twice). Beauty
here is not an aesthetic quality, but a phenomenological
one. The defeat of the Titans by the Olympians marks the
moment when a cosmogony fails, and the images by which
a world could be understood are no longer invested by
the divine power by which they, and the world they repre-
sented, subsisted. Beauty here unfolds from essence, an outward appearance of an inner, hidden, occult order; beauty
hints at the structure of the world. Keats places himself in
a position of extraordinary witness: a place where beauty
is the very record of cosmogonic crisis. Life and death are
included in this crisis. More astonishingly, the images by
which poetry values life and death are included in this crisis.

This crisis is imaginary.

That is, this crisis occurs in the imagination's most profound depths—there where the Titanic gods still linger, de-
feated in their strengthless strength, deathlessly dead, and
the Olympians etch in daylight's new order. Imagination,
Keats knows, cannot be other than the fundamental battle-
ground.

Imagination in crisis becomes Keats's most consistent theme in the letters of 1819. "I have been always till now almost as careless of this world as a fly; my troubles were all of the Imagination."[1] "Imaginary grievances have always been more my torment than real ones."[2] "I feel I can bear real ills better than imaginary ones."[3] His real grievances are largely financial. He has no money, and George's prospects in America have taken a severely downward turn. Keats ponders giving up poetry. He thinks about becoming a hat-maker, of returning to medicine, of writing "professionally," and of earning money and fame by composing a play with Charles Brown. He feels the real world of mundane concerns press into and against the "thousand worlds" in which he has come to dwell, and those worlds gained by imagination's work are planet-struck by the presence of the daily one. The world of high romance — faeries and shepherds — and the epic world of Titans and Olympians cannot wholly withstand the encroachment of this everyday reality whose impact scatters imaginary worlds back into the chaos from which they emerged.

The Odes occur within this difficulty. Keats's feel for his own imagination is undergoing a crisis marked by the *Hyperion* poems, but unable to be solved by them. The Odes chart out, as much as such terrain can be charted out, the agonizing process of Keats's imagination confronting — and being confronted by — "this world" he can no longer treat as carelessly as a fly. They present the awful middle ground in which a world made real by imagination's ardent pursuit collides with a world that denies ardor as its required source — a world that says back to the poet, "I am, with or without you, real." Keats can no longer afford to take for granted the holiness of imagination's worlding work. There is an effort made in the Odes to initiate him into a new realization of imagination's powers, one that requires him to question completely his previous thoughts — Imagination as "Adam's dream," to wake is to find it true — and ask after other possibilities, including one in which poetry exists to

> . . . save
> Imagination from the sable charm
> And dumb enchantment.[4]

In these lines we can read those dangers inherent in imaginative work: an enchantment that secretly teaches us to revel in pleasures that forsake the actual world, that charm us from the fact of our own lives. Keats feels pressing upon him the ethical threat inside imagination's creative promise. Keats sees that the poem might be the place in which imagination must be saved from itself. It is a curious agony that must first create its own pain to find any ease. The Odes are a record of this agony — this agony seeking within itself the means of its own release.

Part of Keats's agony is that he has fallen in love with Fanny Brawne.

The "vaporous shroud" Keats found obstructing his vision of heaven and hell atop Ben Nevis, the mist he found filling the fathomless chasms, have become for Keats an aspect of his poetic condition. He sets down to write whenever "I find myself growing vapourish."[5] He does not write as a lesser poet might, to dispel the fog; he writes to enter it. That fog arises, miasmic, out of erotic turmoil. Keats writes to Fanny: "I must remain some days in a Mist. I see you through a Mist, as I dare say you do me by this time. . . . The thousand images I have had pass through my brain — my uneasy spirits, my unguess'd fate — all spread as a veil between me and you."[6] Keats admits that his poetic work and its "thousand images" act as a barrier between himself and Fanny. It seems he does not know how to see her as herself, outside of those erotic magnifications with which poetry lenses his eyes — a supernal vision that is, in the actual world, a mist, a veil, an obstruction. "Mist" and "veil" cannot be assumed to be wholly negative in their connotation, though one feels a weary despair in the letter. As much as "mist" and "veil" obstruct clear vision, it is also into such obscurity that what is holy and in need of protection steps. What is hidden but sensed, a presence felt but not fully discernable, agonizes thought's reach for clear sight with the soul's need for an ob-scure world in which what is holy must be a felt presence, imperfectly seen because perfectly essential.

This ambivalence forces revelation and secrecy into an uneasy alliance. Keats describes the difference between himself and Byron as "he describes what he sees, I describe what I imagine. Mine is the hardest task."[7] Part of that dif-ficulty, made so present in the Odes, is that Keats must learn to include the veil's intervention in what he imagines visible; to be honest, to be accurate, he must include the mist in his vision.

Riddled with such contradictions, the Odes present no proof of Keats's poetic endeavor, but offer a better gift: the continual demonstration of his doubt. Their power is, in part, their unparalleled ability to critique their own work even as they further it. Doubt here is a fertile, if ago-nized ground. No aspect of Keats's poetic epistemology is secreted away from the force of his inquiry. His love for Fanny exacerbates this questioning. The erotic realities of love, of body helplessly in magnetic tow to other body, of procreative impulses that mimic creative ones, force Keats to admit to worldly facts that seem to oppose poetic ones. Love brings him torment. "I cannot bear the pain of being happy," he writes, fearing that happiness would remove him from those difficulties that unfold into poems. He writes, "My love has made me selfish." He writes the sentence twice in the same letter. "My love has made me selfish."[8] It is a breathtaking moment, for in the phrase is a signal that the man who has claimed that the "poetical character" is with-out self, has no identical nature, and so is the least poetical thing in nature, has so been affected by the fervency of his love that his selfless substance has been stamped into self. This man who looks "upon fine Phrases like a Lover"[9] is himself now a lover, and poetic erotics and personal erotics provide for Keats, in Keats, the ancient *agon*.

Agon refers to those contests, those struggles—from wrestling to war—so valued in ancient Greek culture. As Debra Hawhee notes in *Bodily Arts: Rhetoric and Athletics in Ancient Greece*, *agon* speaks to "the place where wars were won or lost (or, for that matter, happened at all), the reasons gods and goddesses came into being, the context for the emergence of philosophy and art, and even, according to Hesiod, the reason crops grew." She goes on: "In the name and spirit of the *agon*, bodies not only came together, they *became* bodies, bodies capable of action . . ."[10]

The Odes are Keats's *agon*.

Indolence; or, The First Seen Shades Return

In spring, the loamy earth loosening from winter's grip, all quickening, Keats struggles with his most common complaint again: "I have written nothing, and almost read nothing, but I must turn over a new leaf."[11] That new leaf hearkens back to the "sensitive leaf on the hot hand of thought."[12] Linking them together not only connects the wish for greater discipline with the turning over of a new page, but that page is itself a leaf, and turned over, it falls on the fever of the previous page. "I dread as much as a Plague the idle fever of two months more without any fruit."[13] Indolence puts at stake extraordinary opposites: plague or plenty. Fever tends toward illness, the outward sign of inner waste. It also calls to mind a heat higher than the mind's native temperature, a secret solar force that like the sun brings the seed to blossom and, burning feverishly, pushes the blossom early through the bloom. In the proper indolent fit, plague inverts into passion, a feeling so fervent it seems that to write a poem one need only press a page's leaf against the forehead.

The physicality of the image continues Keats's critique of intelligence as a poem's primary source. "I am three and twenty with little knowledge and middling intellect. It is true that in the height of enthusiasm I have been cheated into some fine passages, but that is nothing."[14] Underneath the self-critique and denigration of his previous work's finest moments, Keats's mention of enthusiasm's creative charge opens a concern that "Ode on Indolence" initiates, and of which each subsequent Ode inquires further. The Odes record enthusiasm's complications. The etymology of the word is telling: to be possessed by a god. Keats seeks not simply inspiration, but enthusiasm — a state of fevered apprehension, where possession and perception are aspects of one another, not the work of the solitary witness, but of the poet asking to see through a god's eyes even as he looks through his own.

The task seems so absurd as to be futile. That futility may explain the crippling indolence he feels; it also explains the indolence out of which springs the first Ode:

> There is a great difference between an easy and an uneasy indolence. An indolent day—fill'd with speculations even of an unpleasant colour—is bearable and even pleasant alone, when one's thoughts cannot find out anything better in the world and experience has told us that locomotion is no change . . .[15]

Keats goes on to speak of one such day, an experience gained from refusing labor's motion:

> My passions are all asleep from my having slumbered till nearly eleven and weakened the animal fibre all over me to a delightful sensation about three degrees on this side of faintness. If I had teeth of pearl and the breath of lilies I should call it languor, but as I am I must call it Laziness. In this state of effeminacy the fibres of the brain are relaxed in common with the rest of the body, and to such a happy degree that pleasure has no show of enticement and pain no unbearable frown. Neither Poetry, nor Ambition, nor Love have any alertness of countenance as they pass by me; they seem rather like three figures on a greek vase—a Man and two women—whom no one but myself could distinguish in their disguisement. This is the only happiness and is a rare instance of advantage in the body overpowering the Mind.[16]

Indolence is a curious experience, one that seems to deny itself as experience; and the indolent self is one who has both the sense of self and the selflessness of sense. Indolence lazily demolishes the binaries of deliberate life, so that the mind eases into the body and becomes the body; the body also becomes the mind, and to feel a breeze blow over the skin is profound thought, and a proverb is a matter for the pulse.

―――――――

When the gods arrive, when those "first seen shades return," Keats says, "they were strange to me."[17]

> One morn before me were three figures seen,
>   With bowed necks, and joined hands, side-faced;
> And one behind the other stepp'd serene,
>   In placid sandals, and in white robes graced:
> They pass'd, like figures on a marble urn,
>   When shifted round to see the other side[18]

Their strangeness isn't simply ascribable to the marvel of the vision. Keats feels most troubled that in his indolent languor, he did not know who the figures are:

> How is it, shadows, that I knew ye not?
>   How came ye muffled in so hush a masque?
> Was it a silent deep-disguised plot
>   To steal away, and leave without a task
> My idle days? Ripe was the drowsy hour;
>   The blissful cloud of summer-indolence
>   Benumbed my eyes; my pulse grew less and less;
> Pain had no sting, and pleasure's wreath no flower.
>   O, why did ye not melt, and leave my sense
>   Unhaunted quite of all but—nothingness?[19]

The three figures appear to Keats at the very moment when his senses are about to relent into senselessness, when the barest vestige of consciousness succumbs to dream. A vision interrupts his slipping away into dream's visions. This "benumbed" state seems prerequisite for much of the experience the Odes offer. Keats suggests that the mind must grow heedless of the senses for enthusiastic vision to occur. He also suggests that when that vision does occur, it is as troubling as it is miraculous. Vision comes, it may be, with a threat.

That threat, that "silent deep-disguised plot," is to "steal away, and leave without a task / My idle days." It is a strange ambiguity deep within indolence's nature to which Keats calls our attention. He fears these as yet unknown figures have come to steal the worth of his idleness; that is, he fears they have come to steal the stuff of the dreams he was about to fall into. His initial instinct is to distrust the figures. The task of his idle days is to find within himself those images that appear as if of themselves in a dream and, gleaned from dreams, come of use in a poem. But these figures refuse Keats the "nothingness" by which he wants to be haunted — a nothingness inside the mind, or self, or body. A poet cannot merely be self-haunted. There are more valid forms of nothingness by which he must be confronted. Where Keats expected to lose himself in sleep, he finds himself enthused — this is not a willing choice. By the "third time pass'd they by,"[20] Keats recognizes the divinities turning about him, a recognition enthusiasm alone offers. Before him, as described in the letter to his brother George and sister-in-law Georgiana, are Love, Ambition, and "my demon Poesy." Keats has before him not only the figure of his own daemonic genius; his genius has come with companions.

Genius comes and makes demands, and its demands are difficult. With every turning of the ode, wherein each stanza presents another cycle of the three figures, Keats is called into response and recognition he is reluctant to accept. In fact, he seems most hopeful that they will leave him alone so he may return to his "drowsy hour": "A third time came they by; — alas! wherefore?"[21] Once Keats realizes the figures are not there to steal his dreams from him, he assumes they have come to "embroider" his sleep with dreams. But their dance is not to lull him into sweeter visions than their own presence offers. That presence, this vision, introduces

Keats to a form of enthusiasm all the Odes depend upon. Keats wants to abandon—or more accurately, Keats wants to be abandoned by—the agony that Love, Ambition, and Poesy force him to recognize. That agony, in the "Ode on Indolence," is the three figures themselves. What Keats cannot help but recognize is that each figure also bears his own countenance, and when they turn their "side-faced" gaze directly at him, he recognizes each because he sees with his eyes his own eyes staring back. They confront him with the nature of his own desire.

Genius has now come to its fullest pressure in Keats's work. The effort of the three figures is to face Keats; but they face him with his own face—those aspects of his identity he would find life easier for never seeing. His desire for them to leave is also a desire to flee from himself, to step away from poetry's demands into a poem-like activity, the dream within the dream of the self. But the self is no dream. The self is called out by Genius into a dance that shatters sleep's repose. The image that bears this awakening is most striking:

> The open casement press'd a new-leaved vine;
> Let in the budding warmth and throstle's lay;
> O shadows! 'twas a time to bid farewell![22]

The domestic image, the window, opens—that opening likewise is a token of the opening of the self, a synecdoche for the eye as it opens rather than closes, and sleep is put away. The last stanza of the poem pretends this is not true, that "Ye cannot raise / My head cool-bedded in the flowery grass," but we have the poem itself as evidence to the contrary. The eye opens and presses against the new-leaved vine: it feels what it sees. It opens and the thrush's song comes pouring in, as if vision also listens. The shadows have done their work despite the poet's resistance. The open windows of "Ode to Psyche" and the bird's song of "Ode to a Nightingale" occur first in indolence. Genius brings them as gifts. These gifts are difficult. To receive them is to be put to work. To write the poem we read, Keats ended his indolence. The work costs exactly the vision. The poem wants this not to be true—but it is. The poet wants this not to be true—that the writing of the poem ends the experience inspiring it—but it is.

Psyche; or,
The Wreath'd Trellis of a Working Brain

Keats begins "Ode to Psyche" with an invocation that is also an apology:

> O Goddess! hear these tuneless numbers, wrung
>> By sweet enforcement and remembrance dear,
> And pardon that thy secrets should be sung
>> Even into thine own soft-conched ear[23]

The ode is addressed to Psyche, the goddess Keats would honor. He sings back to her immortal ear her own story, reveals back to her her own secrets. This redundancy contains a threat. He knows that such reverence risks blaspheming the very figure of his devotion, for in speaking to the goddess Keats also speaks to us. He has come to a sense of the poem — and more largely, of poetry — as entwined with fundamental ironies. Inescapable inversions seem a primary consequence of poetry as a phenomenal practice. Poetry, Keats has learned, can keep no secrets; it shows the secret forth. The cost of devotion to a goddess is to keep silent about those mysteries devotion reveals. But a poem keeps no words silent. It forces into appearance all that should remain hidden in the blank page's nothingness. A poem expressing faith betrays the figure of that faith — it cannot be helped. And so Keats apologizes to Psyche for calling her into being — the very work of *agony*.

Why Keats risks such betrayal, why he speaks of an experience the very expression of which may preclude him from experiencing again (the gods not taking kindly to trespass, see Actaeon, see Pentheus) will occupy many of the Odes, each subtly altering the conditions of its questioning. The questioning condition in "Ode to Psyche" springs out from "Ode on Indolence." His repose tending toward thoughtlessness that Love, Ambition, and Poesy interrupt with their appearance becomes here a far more difficult state to achieve: "I wander'd in a forest thoughtlessly."[24] If not wholly abandoning indolence as a primary creative ground, Keats now suspects he must find an action that can still maintain indolence's nature—that admixture of mind and body so complete no separation can be meaningfully found. A "thoughtless wandering" enacts Keats's ongoing critique of poetry of "palpable design." The requirement for actual discovery is the complete abandonment of that intent which prescribes what the poet will find. The most that can be done, Keats suggests, is to walk into the woods on purpose; but in the woods, purpose dissolves into bewilderment's wilder possibilities. Keats must become lost. Thoughts mark a path the mind knows how to follow, paths so well-worn they preclude the existence of the forest they cross. Vision begins where direction ends, for then one must see the unmarked clearings to move. And what Keats sees is a vision erotic, Psyche and Cupid, in intimate embrace:

> They lay calm-breathing on the bedded grass;
>   Their arms embraced, and their pinions too;
>   Their lips touch'd not, but had not bade adieu,
> As if disjoined by soft-handed slumber[25]

Keats has accomplished a poetic feat he has longed for from his earliest poems: he has entered the very chamber of erotic bliss, witness to what none should witness, save the lovers themselves. Vision is a sacred trespass, and the poet must learn to accept that he is a seer. What he sees, he must speak. And to speak risks revelation—not merely of his own trespassing presence, but revelation of the goddess's dearest secrecy.

Keats offers an insightful critique of the writing habits of Charles Brown, his close friend with whom he occasionally lived, who was then writing a story "of his old woman and the Devil": "The fact is, it is a Libel on the Devil and as that person is Brown's Muse, look ye, if he libels his own Muse how can he expect to write."[26] The implied difference is that Keats writes so as to revere his Muse, and his Muse is Psyche.

The realization is telling. Psyche isn't simply a figure of the soul. Her mythic ordeal prefigures other key aspects of Keats's poetic epistemology. Those tests with which Venus torments her—the separation of seeds, the collection of the golden wool, the box of infernal sleep—reveal the way in which soul interacts with the self it animates. Psyche's gift—like that of the simpleton heroes of many fairy tales—resides paradoxically in her lack of self-sufficiency. She knows what she is not able to accomplish herself, and in gracious return, the world offers her help. Ants come to sift the seeds into order. The river-god offers advice to gather the wool from the thorn-trees while the golden sheep sleep in the shade. Cupid returns to wipe the sleep from her eyes. The soul seems to remind the self of its inability, its insufficiency. The soul may undermine the ego in such a way that will relents and opens—as Keats's imaginative flowers open to the bee—to some reciprocity in the world that lends its limitless source to the self's very problem: the lack of resource in the self's own hand. Soul allows self to accept itself as absence. So might Keats's Muse remind him, this poet who claims the poet isn't "selfless," but has no self.

But "Ode to Psyche" does not explore the entire myth. Keats encounters Cupid and Psyche in the thoughtless woods, in embrace so intimate they seem to breathe each other's breath and need no other air. Keats conflates the beginning and the ending of the myth, when Psyche and Cupid first become lovers, and long after, when Psyche becomes a goddess and Cupid's immortal wife. This erotic cycle offers Keats a pattern to explain his own poetic concerns, and much of the real beauty in "Ode to Psyche" results from it being the fullest unfolding of Keats's poetic yet seen within his poems.

Venus sends Cupid down to glance Psyche with an arrow so that she'll fall in love with a hideous creature — a pre-emptive strike against the woman's beauty. Psyche sleeps with her window open, and though it's night and in the room there is no light, Cupid comes invisible. As he holds his nocked arrow ready, Psyche awakes, and her staring straight into the eyes of the invisible god so startles him that he wounds himself with his arrow's edge. Cupid falls in love, and Psyche leaves her window open at night to allow her lover to visit; the ongoing promise of the erotic encounter is threatened only by Cupid's warning that she never try to discover his true form. Psyche's sisters, jealous of her love, convince her to set a trap. She does. She lights a lamp to look at the god as he sleeps, and when a drop of oil falls on his shoulder, he awakes — the god awakes betrayed — and out the window of his nightly arrival, he flees.

In the early part of Psyche's tale, Keats finds a template for his own poetic experience. The poet, like Psyche, impossibly recognizes the invisible god's presence, finds within the world something the world itself should not allow, and in doing so, creates a new place — a meeting ground, a bower, a bridal chamber — whose symbolic nature allows two separate worlds to join in erotic consummation. The poet finds on the blank page the wedding bed's white sheets. The promise of the poem is that a world entirely mortal is redeemed back into eternity by the mere recognition that eternity exists, as do the gods, as do the eyes of the gods staring invisibly into our own, as Keats knows as he seeks his "hethen" faith.[27] But Keats also knows such union cannot last long. He knows that Psyche will seek to see the god who loves her, and this need for visibility betrays the erotic bond that keeps linked separate worlds. The poem is a work of revelation. The cost of showing us who read it what in it we see is exactly the loss of what we see, what we would want always to see, a desire that cannot be fulfilled in honest ways when ethics and erotics are, as they are in Keats, one. The god flees, and the poet follows; the poet follows and endures his tests. The only evidence of success is wandering thoughtlessly into the next poem.

This vision that Keats thoughtlessly stumbles upon startles him into a new realization, one that alters how a poem's work might be perceived. Actually, a pun might serve better to speak to the point: Keats has a vision that *altars* the poem. Troubled by the fact that Psyche, this "latest born and loveliest vision far / Of all Olympus' faded hierarchy" has no temple to honor her, no "virgin-choir to make delicious moan / Upon the midnight hours," Keats nominates himself to be "thy priest."[28] Inside this service is an extraordinary audacity, one reminiscent of an infant god determined to be included among Olympus's pantheon. The baby Hermes — trickster god of poetry, alphabet, and gambling — steals and sacrifices Apollo's sacred cattle, and though the burning offering torments him with hunger, he will eat none. Instead, he includes his own name in his prayers, vaulting himself heavenward. Keats isn't exactly apotheosizing himself, but he is reducing the consequence of his trespass by making himself — as poet — the caretaker of the sacred vision, and as much as the poem itself risks betraying the goddess he worships, it is in the poem alone that her divinity is recognized and held holy.

Against the poem's inherent, expressive threat, Keats offers another paradigm:

> Yes, I will be thy priest, and build a fane
>   In some untrodden region of my mind,
> Where branched thoughts, new grown with pleasant pain,
>   Instead of pines shall murmur in the wind:

Far, far around shall those dark-clustr'd trees
   Fledge the wild-ridged mountains steep by steep;
And there by zephyrs, streams, and birds, and bees,
   The moss-lain Dryads shall be lull'd to sleep;
And in the midst of this wide quietness
A rosy sanctuary will I dress
With the wreath'd trellis of a working brain,
   With buds, and bells, and stars without a name,
With all the gardener Fancy e'er could feign,
   Who breeding flowers, will never breed the same:
And there shall be for thee all soft delight
   That shadowy thought can win,
A bright torch, and a casement ope at night,
   To let the warm Love in![29]

All Keats externalizes in "Ode on Indolence," he interiorizes in "Ode to Psyche." Both poems adhere to a law of radical reciprocity. To turn inwards in the former, Keats casts out the visiting "figures" that interrupt his slipping into benumbed sleep. In the latter, Keats wanders thoughtlessly into the forest, and his reaction to what he finds there outside of himself is to create within his "living brain" a dwelling for the goddess to live. It is as if Keats, "by my own eyes inspired,"[30] has discovered a way both to speak back to the goddess her own secrets (and so betray them to us) and to create a new realm of secrecy within the telling itself, a silence beneath the words, a silence the words don't interrupt, but like the new "branched thoughts," a silence the words embower and protect.

Keats thinks so as to create in his mind a "wide quietness," an "untrodden region," an area where thought cannot enter, but which thought guards. Thought becomes enthusiasm's house, for it is within its varied sanctuary the goddess reclines. Keats's role as poet becomes beautifully simple, for the deep virtue of the role has little do with the poems he writes. It has everything to do with "[a] bright torch, and a casement ope at night." For the open casement must be the poet's own open eyes. A remarkable reversal is the signal achievement of the poem. The wilderness is within the poet's house, not without it. Domesticity has been inverted. Keats keeps his eyes open, keeps the torch of his intelligence burning, not to think in any normal sense of the word, but to see so as to think, to perceive so as to give fancy a material to construct forever "breeding flowers" that "will never breed the same." Most importantly, and perhaps the germ of the poetic that allows the subsequent Odes their unquestionable greatness, his eyes are open so Cupid can fly in and find his love, and in the thoughtless penetralium of the poet's mind, Soul and Love consummate forever their nuptial bond.

Melancholy; or,
The Rainbow of the Salt Sand-Wave

Keats begins "Ode on Melancholy" in a chant to resist his instinct. That instinct, as in the previous two Odes, impels him toward indolence, and the senselessness that indolence, Lethe-like, brings.

> No, no, go not to Lethe, neither twist
>   Wolf's-bane, tight-rooted, for its poisonous wine;
> Nor suffer thy pale forehead to be kiss'd
>   By nightshade, ruby grape of Proserpine;
> Make not your rosary of yew-berries,
>   Nor let the beetle, nor death-moth be
>   Your mournful Psyche . . .[31]

As the highly stressed charge of "No, no, go not" relents into a lyric dominated by sounds of ritual mourning—the almost sobbing long "oo," cut by the tongue hitting the back of the teeth to make the "t," and the plosive expulsion of "b" and "p"—Keats creates within a soundscape of sorrow and sorrow's rage a poem that returns to the dominating figure of "Ode to Psyche." Keats's goddess, his Muse, no longer is Psyche herself, but a metaphor that stands in for Psyche—a beetle or a death-moth. This shift from the poet as priest who contains in his head divine essence, to poet as one who must resist the very figures of speech that mark his brilliance, speaks of "Ode on Melancholy" as marking yet another radical shift in how the poet approaches what work the poem itself undertakes. Psyche, divine figure of Keats's erotic epistemology, seems to have fled as her husband had fled, out the open window of the poet's eyes—and so the poet scans the world for substitution. The opening stanza of "Ode on Melancholy" sings into Keats's godless crisis, and the stanzas to follow record how he responds to this death-like condition—save that death would remove him from the pain of the crisis of which he strives so hard to remain sensible.

His instinct, as so often, is toward sensation. Opposed to his fear of craving the very death he should resist, he links *death* and *eros* into mutually embracing opposites. He gluts his "sorrow on a morning rose,"[32] but instinct presses on his mind in other ways.

> For in wild nature the Hawk would lose his Breakfast of Robins and the Robin his of Worms. The Lion must starve as well as the swallow. The greater part of Men make their way with the same instinctiveness, the same unwandering eye from their purposes, the same animal eagerness as the Hawk. The Hawk wants a Mate, so does the Man. Look at them both; they set about it and procure one in the same manner. They want both a nest and they both set about one in the same manner; they get their food in the same manner. The noble animal Man for his amusement smokes his pipe; the Hawk balances about the Clouds—that is the only difference of their leisures. This it is that makes the Amusement of Life to a speculative Mind. I go among the Fields and catch a glimpse of a stoat or a field mouse peeping out of the withered grass. The creature hath a purpose and its eyes are bright with it. I go amongst the buildings of a city and I see a Man hurrying along—to what? The Creature has a purpose and his eyes are bright with it.[33]

Keats sees that our nature pulls us into our senses, and instinct undergirds reason in ways as complicated as how beauty undergirds consideration—that is, the fault line in the fundament sets the structure atremble. Against reason's denial of death—the sense that Truth outlasts the life that grasps it—instinct enters into death as a force that furthers life ("they get their food in the same manner"). That instinct that leads the Hawk and the Man to the violence of his breakfast also leads them to seek a mate—that is, appetite links hunger and desire, and instinct, even the instinct toward leisure, includes within it a force of *wanting* that cannot be easily denied.

The "eye is bright" with what it wants. And when one wants to feed — erotically, essentially — on the beloved other, then instinct pushes the poet into realms of profound contradiction. Keats, in the same letter, writes:

> Even here, though I myself am pursuing the same instinctive course as the veriest human animal you can think of, I am however young writing at a random, straining at particles of light in the midst of a great darkness without knowing the bearing of any one assertion of any one opinion. Yet may I not in this be free from sin?[34]

Something in Keats — the poet Keats, or Keats as Poet — knows his eye is bright with the instinct to seek after brightness. He hints at such in a letter to Fanny Brawne, linking yet again the erotic with poetry's epistemological desires (not knowledge exactly, but a coming to know how one knows): "I want a brighter word than bright."[35] He wants such a word because the brightness of the eye is what he feeds upon: "What would I not give tonight for the gratification of my eyes alone?"[36] That gratification is complex, unable to pull apart the impulse toward beauty from the impulse toward death, as if the "particles of light" can gratify only opposed to the "great darkness" against which they show.

> I have two luxuries to brood over in my walks, your Loveliness and the hour of my death. O that I could have possession of them both in the same minute. I hate the world; it batters too much the wings of my self-will, and would I could take a sweet poison from your lips to send me out of it.[37]

The pinpoint precision of this double luxury — *eros* and *thanatos* — crash one against another as does the collision that causes the "rainbow of the salt sand-wave."[38] It is only by virtue of opposed forces colliding that the brightness Keats instinctually seeks can be found, the rainbow in the broken sea's spray.

> Or if thy mistress some rich anger shows,
>   Emprison her soft hand, and let her rave,
>   And feed deep, deep upon her peerless eyes.[39]

He finds a human depth in those eyes, even if it's a depth in turmoil. Keats has transitioned from the three visages meeting his indolent look, from opening his own eyes to keep Psyche hidden in ever-new blooms, to seeking a returning gaze that is pointedly human. It is for the human that he wishes to stay awake.

But the mistress "dwells with Beauty—Beauty that must die."[40] Despite the vision of the rainbow's brightness leaping out of the sea crashing into the rock, Keats finds allegorical figures returning to presence in the poem, obstructing the luxurious melancholy of his gratifying gaze. The presence of the gods that for so long have been the highest hope of Keats's fevered work arrive in the third stanza as a profound threat to the human moment—as painful and awkward as it is—preceding their arrival. They also arrive with a terrible consequence, one that strikes the ear on hearing it without fate's brute weight. Again, the letters predict the dilemma the poem reveals. Preceding his thoughts on instinct, Keats ponders the nature of circumstance:

> While we are laughing the seed of some trouble is put into the wide arable land of events. While we are laughing it sprouts, it grows and suddenly bears a poison fruit which we must pluck.[41]

This sense of happiness forming within itself a poison we have no choice but to consume is mirrored in his wish expressed to Fanny Brawne regarding the circumstance of his life: "would I could take a sweet poison from your lips to send me out of it."[42] This image returns in the "Ode on Melancholy."

> And Joy, whose hand is ever at his lips,
>   Bidding adieu; and aching Pleasure nigh,
>   Turning to poison while the bee-mouth sips:
> Ay, in the very temple of Delight
>   Veil'd Melancholy has her sovran shrine,
>   Though seen of none save him whose strenuous
>   tongue
>   Can burst Joy's grape against his palate fine[43]

Keats has found out how death secrets itself inside every bliss, even the bliss of poetry, even the bliss of love. His wish, as expressed in *Endymion*, of the poem as guide to "how to consummate all" has found within it the darker image first encountered in his verse letter to Reynolds when he "saw / Too far into the sea"[44] where all that consumes is also consumed, and this forevermore. The eye, that dark flower open to the sun's light, consumes what peers into it. In vision there is this threat: that what we see we feed upon, and brightness distills down into poison, as potent as any contradictory essence. Here Keats's background in the medical pharmacy collides wholly with the ancient *pharmakon*, where poison and cure are one and the same, and language itself bears inside it the fever from which it also seeks ease. Keats can no longer assume that poetry is simply, without irony, "a friend to man."

Nightingale; or, Fled Is That Music

What in "Ode on Melancholy" Keats denied himself, he has — willingly or not, we don't know — partaken of in "Ode to a Nightingale":

> My heart aches, and a drowsy numbness pains
>> My sense, as though of hemlock I had drunk,
> Or emptied some dull opiate to the drains
>> One minute past, and Lethe-wards had sunk[45]

Keats feels in himself some death-like stealing away of sensation. "Hemlock" not only implies that this "drowsy numbness" results from his own self-destructive hand, but links the opening crisis of the poem with Socrates's death. That link bears importance in framing the Nightingale's peculiar agony. Socrates drinks hemlock not only because he has been sentenced to die, but because death is for him a test of his own thinking, a demonstration — startling in its irreversibility — of the soul's immortality. Socrates can die because death will allow his soul a greater wakefulness, a return to that pure Being of which mortal life but feeds on the vestiges and dregs. Keats's poems have long mirrored such a relation to Being, opening within themselves visions of eternity the poet — missing identity, missing character — enters as the gift writing's labor offers as recompense. But poetry's gift has become complicated; the Odes are the demonstration of these complications.

That alteration in Keats's thinking can perhaps best be felt in his changing relationship to identity. The famous passage from his long letter to George and Georgiana Keats is so fine it must be quoted at length:

> Call the world if you Please "The vale of Soul-making."
> Then you will find out the use of the world (I am speak-

ing now in the highest terms for human nature admitting it to be immortal, which I will here take for granted for the purpose of showing a thought which has struck me concerning it). I say 'Soul-making,' Soul as distinguished from an Intelligence. There may be intelligences or sparks of the divinity in millions, but they are not Souls till they acquire identities, till each one is personally itself. Intelligences are atoms of perception; they know and they see and they are pure, in short they are God. How then are Souls to be made? How then are these sparks which are God to have identity given them so as ever to possess a bliss peculiar to each one's individual existence? How, but by the medium of a world like this? This point I sincerely wish to consider because I think it a grander system of salvation than the chrystain religion, or rather it is a system of Spirit-creation. This is effected by three grand materials acting the one upon the other for a series of years. These three Materials are the *Intelligence*, the *human heart* (as distinguished from intelligence or Mind) and the *World* or *Elemental space* suited for the proper action of *Mind and Heart* on each other for the purpose of forming the *Soul* or *Intelligence destined to possess the sense of Identity*. I can scarcely express what I but dimly perceive, and yet I think I perceive it. That you may judge the more clearly I will put it in the most homely form possible. I will call the *world* a School instituted for the purpose of teaching little children to read. I will call the *human heart* the *horn Book* used in that School, and I will call the *Child able to read, the Soul* made from that *school* and its *hornbook*. Do you not see how necessary a World of Pains and troubles is to school an Intelligence and make it a soul? A Place where the heart must feel and suffer in a thousand diverse ways! Not merely is the Heart a Hornbook; it is the Mind's Bible, it is the Mind's experience, it is the teat from which the Mind or intelligence sucks its identity. As various as the Lives of Men are, so various become their Souls, and thus does God make individual beings, Souls, Identical Souls of the sparks of his own essence. This appears to me a faint sketch of a system of Salvation which does not affront our reason and humanity. . . . I will but put you in the place where I began in this series of thoughts; I mean, I began by seeing how man was formed by circumstances, and what are circumstances but touchstones of his heart? And what are touchstones but proovings of his heart? And what are proovings of his heart but fortifiers or alterers of his nature? And what is his altered nature but his soul? And what was his soul before it came into the world and had These provings and alterations and perfectionings? An intelligence — without Identity — and how is this Identity to be made? Through the medium of the Heart. And how is the heart to become this Medium but in a world of Circumstances?[46]

That "world of Circumstances" is likewise — from earlier in the same letter — those cloud-like circumstances whose rain-burst brings to ripeness the "poison fruit which we must pluck." It is the world entire, the fact of the world's matter, its "elemental space" — and it seems that for Keats, the poem can no longer ignore those daily damages that not only afflict the imagination with mortality's splinter, but agonize the poet with identity. This world is also the world of "Ode to a Nightingale" — or, at least, it is half this great ode's world, where the poet feels

> The weariness, the fever, and the fret
>   Here, where men sit and hear each other groan;
> Where palsy shakes a few, sad, last gray hairs,
>   Where youth grows pale, and spectre-thin, and dies;
>   Where but to think is to be full of sorrow
>   And leaden-eyed despairs,
>   Where Beauty cannot keep her lustrous eyes,
>   Or new Love pine at them beyond to-morrow.[47]

As much as Psyche is a figure of Soul, she is also a figure of allegorical Beauty. Love's pining evokes Psyche's husband Eros, but Eros in a world awfully changed, in which the window of his arrival is closed to the god, and Psyche's eyes grow dim in the embowered altar of the poet's mind. The inner sanctum and the outer world cease to connect through the poet's open eyes. Keats must seek a different method by which to return to that world in which Being and Soul are free from the damage this world of circumstances inflicts upon him. "Ode to a Nightingale" is this very story, a story of no conclusion, save the bewilderment of existing as poet and person at once.

It cannot be helped, nor is it wholly negative, that one becomes a person. Against Keats's earlier description of the poet as one who has no identity, he recognizes that living in the actual world—the world where Tom dies, the world where Keats verges on bankruptcy—shapes one not merely into a self, but far more radically, into an "Identical Soul." The very essence that in Socrates frees itself from the diminishments of human limits and returns to the ideal truth of Form becomes in Keats the very fingerprint of selfhood. As one becomes a soul—as the mind learns to read the damage-inscribed heart—one also learns to say "I." To say "I" includes "a bliss peculiar," includes a sense of the erotic so individual as to make love a human capacity and not only a joy reserved for the gods, or those humans who venture into Arcadian fields with imaginative force. But this "grander system of salvation" threatens Keats's poetic epistemology. To learn to read his own heart, to become an individual soul, requires that he risk severing his connection to that lack of self which allows him to become Saturn or Ops or a roomful of schoolchildren desperate to escape their dull lesson. This "homely" form of his theory of "Spirit-creation" shows how identity is shaped by the breakdown of the boundary between the external world and the internal self. The world inscribes a damage onto the heart's hornbook, and these words — words the person alone could not write, words that are not the result of imaginative effort — teach the student-mind to read. Our innermost is marked by the outermost. Becoming fluent in such circumstantial damage creates in us a soul that is a resource within, and against, the "poison fruit" we have no choice but to pluck and eat.

To place Keats's sense of "Spirit-creation" as it leads to identity next to his understanding of the "camelion poet"[48] requires its own act of negative capability. The very ability to compose a poem for Keats rests in a lack of self so complete that he is towed magnetically into the existence of others; now, at the same time, he is learning to be in the world in ways he had previously maligned.

> I have of late been moulting — not for fresh feathers and wings — they are gone — and in their stead I hope to have a pair of patient sublunary legs. I have altered, not from a Chrysalis into a butterfly, but the Contrary, having two little loopholes, whence I may look out into the stage of the world . . .[49]

One of the odd and remarkable powers of the Odes, and one that plays itself out in "Ode to a Nightingale" so exquisitely, is their ability to show the poet as double-voiced, double-selfed, person and Poet, and seek a way not to judge between this duality, but to record the ways in which these oppositions coexist, each threatening to cancel out the reality of the other. What is at stake in the poem is the very ability to write the poem.

Perhaps it is worth assuming that the darkness from which Keats "can scarcely express what I but dimly perceive, and yet I think I perceive it" is the same night's gloom in "Ode to a Nightingale" in which the poet "cannot see what flowers are at my feet." The nature of Keats's genius completely confounds perception and thought to the degree that thinking itself is sensational, has a "feel," even if the feel is not to feel. That faculty is here benumbed, save that the poet hears "In some melodious plot / Of beechen green, and shadows numberless" the "light-winged Dryad of the trees."[50] "Light-winged" is so quietly a synesthetic phrase. The bird is nimble; it can fly into the darker dark of the underbrush away from the listening poet. But its wings are also a source of light, a means of making perceptible the world from which the drab bird sings. Where the nightingale alights, it also lights — a world the poet knows exists only through the nightingale singing from it in "full-throated ease."

In calling the bird a Dryad, Keats posits it immediately within an immortal context, and so its song is the very song he has yearned to sing himself: an eternal song. That song, by its very nature, excludes the knowledge Keats would himself love dearly to forget — that identity circumstance has given him, the complicated burden of being a self. Over the course of the ode, the relation of the bird to the song it sings changes in important ways. The bird as Dryad shifts to a different kind of immortality:

> Thou wast not born for death, immortal Bird!
>   No hungry generations tread thee down;
> The voice I hear this passing night was heard
>   In ancient days by emperor and clown:
> Perhaps the self-same song that found a path
>   Through the sad heart of Ruth, when, sick for home,
>   She stood in tears amid the alien corn;
>   The same that oft-times hath
>   Charm'd magic casements, opening on the foam
>   Of perilous seas, in faery lands forlorn.[51]

The bird is not immortal in body, but immortal in song. The generations of nightingales are born into the song they each sing, and that song is unchanging over time, innate, instinctual, offering to all who have ever heard it the same melancholy comfort of its tune. But we must also see that this song is no song of knowledge. It is a song without expression, a song without words. The nature of its immortal life cannot be separated from the fact of its wordlessness. Its wings light up a world that can be seen only as long as what fills the eye leaves the mouth bereft — a poetic crisis of deepest magnitude.

Keats has long been a poet desirous of learning how to withstand the ambiguities of dimness. The unseen nightingale sings out of darkness, sings out of darkness its ancient, immortal song. Keats listens to it as a man who says "I"; he wants to listen to it as a poet who has no self to say "I." He fears that if the bird should near him it will succumb to the knowledge of the world that has impinged upon his own poetic nature, a damage that makes the writing of the poem an impossible thing. (The deep irony embedded within "Ode to a Nightingale" occurs in the sense that the poem records the impossibility of its own existence — it is a poem that cannot be written.) Keats's solution is to scare the bird

> Away! away! for I will fly to thee,
>   Not charioted by Bacchus and his pards,
> But on the viewless wings of Poesy[52]

Keats relies on his sense that what is real becomes so only by ardent pursuit. He scares away the bird so that he can follow it on poetry's "viewless wings." This pursuit of the bird is also a pursuit of that absolute poem which contains a world it also cannot utter, a space of essence, of Being. Keats's greatness, in part, resides exactly in this command that the bird flee, this realization — deep as the nerves and blood in the mind — that says he must pursue what he wants to be real. Keats wants to follow the song the bird sings, the song the bird lives eternally within, and to describe that pursuit as he does so. The poem may be no more than a record of that pursuit, dependent on that pursuit to exist. It is itself a redefinition of the thinking it is also a demonstration of, a devoted leap into that chasm between immortal bird and mortal man, abyss from which Being itself cannot deny that thinking almost describes it.

That thoughtful description requires that sensation alter. Within the Platonic undergirding of the poem lurks a mythological sense of death and rebirth. The river Lethe divides in halves opposite forms of existence, life from death — the very line the poet is fated to cross and re-cross. When a soul is called back into the world, it drinks from the river Lethe, and forgets the universal truths of which it had been part, and informs the body with a vitality that lacks the absolute knowledge that in death had been its own. Keats has reversed this process. He is in life, in the world, an identical soul. His Lethe-wards sinking implies a forgetting of life that allows him to follow the nightingale into death's ancient peace, a desire to exchange world for World. Keats wants to flee the agony of a mortal life composed of those momentary eternities in none of which can we dwell. He acts as he once wrote of Apollo; he "die[s] into life."[53]

Such metamorphosis rearranges Keats's dearest poetic modes. Sensation itself alters. The Lethe-like drift not only turns blank those memories of the weary, fevered world, it undoes the means by which that world had been known. Keats's mind extends to the very ends of his nerves. But here, the darkness of the falling night through which the "light-winged" bird sings is a more profound darkness than the absence of the sun's light. Sensation itself is dimmed, diminishing, turning dark — a death-like swoon that within the poem's crisis does not carry within it the assurance of salvation (save for the nightingale's immortal singing). In this darkening world, "[w]here but to think is to be full of sorrow," sensation — as the very root of thought — must derange itself. The synesthetic "light-winged" bird predicts the poet's own change. When the darkness becomes complete, Keats has lost his vision in the most profound of ways: "I cannot see what flowers are at my feet." That loss — a form of death — precedes a remarkable rebirth.

> I cannot see what flowers are at my feet,
>   Nor what soft incense hangs upon the boughs,
> But, in embalmed darkness, guess each sweet
>   Wherewith the seasonable month endows
> The grass, the thicket, and the fruit-tree wild;
>   White hawthorn, and the pastoral eglantine;
>   Fast fading violets cover'd up in leaves;
>   And mid-May's eldest child,
>   The coming musk-rose, full of dewy wine,
>   The murmurous haunt of flies on summer eves.[54]

The subtle mistake made in the second line of the stanza, where "soft incense" is something seen rather than smelled, sparks a mode of sensation that revivifies the "embalmed darkness" of the night. Keats learns to see through another sense; he becomes synesthetic. He breathes in vision, and so can see the flowers in the absolute dark as if the dark did not exist. The miracle of the poem is that sensation itself has grown perceptive. Scent is vision; sound is vision.

This synesthetic mode rescues Keats — at least partially, at least potentially — from this world's sorrow. But where in earlier poems this crescendo would have marked the poem's ultimate achievement, the maturity of the Odes knows that every rescue is also an introduction to a different agony. That agony involves synesthesia shifting from a perceptive mode to a phenomenological one. Keats seeks a method to exist doubly: as Poet and as person. The vision the nightingale shepherds him into isn't the deathless sphere he might have hoped he'd find. He sees "Ruth, when, sick for home, / She stood in tears amid the alien corn." He flies on poetry's viewless wings into a vision of sorrow that lives past the life that experienced it. "Faery lands" are no escape from the sorrow of the "Mind's Bible."

Keats hears a bell ring in a word: forlorn, forlorn. That

too is a gift of synesthesia, a complicated gift, tolling him "back to my sole self." That return to the sole self, so unexpected, so sorrowful, after the accomplishment of becoming more than mere self, of becoming doubled, Poet and person, immortal and mortal, in fairy land and garden, leaves Keats carrying only the confused residue of a genuine confounding. "Do I wake or sleep?" He asks a question he cannot answer.

Urn; or, To What Green Altar

To write the line "Thou still unravish'd bride of quietness" ravishes the quiet bride. Keats opens "Ode on a Grecian Urn" in a dilemma similar to singing Psyche's secrets back into her own "soft-conched ear." Immediately, we find ourselves confronted with possibilities that undermine our assumptions of a poem's relationship to its subject, and a poem's relationship to who wrote it. The poem grows ambivalent. It seems not to serve the needs of self-expression of the one who composed it; it seems to betray in its expression all it would honor with its singing. "Ode on a Grecian Urn" exacerbates the discomfort of these issues as no other poem in Keats's oeuvre does.

The Urn is a burial container; it is meant to hold the ashes of the dead. But as in all great poems, the nature of the palpable object manifests within itself a symbolic complexity always less than, and more than, palpable. That complexity must be felt in all its oddity for the poem's meaning to be fully grasped. Grasped may well be the right word, for one of the aspects that marks the nature of this poem — so different than in the other Odes — is that the Poet is here holding the object of his concern. That object holds within itself, within the images of the brede that circle it, elements of every other Ode. In some profound sense, the Urn contains the other Odes — and so, not only does "Ode on a Grecian Urn" become a poem investigating its own peculiar crisis, but that crisis is composed of the other Odes. The poem asks a question about the practice of writing poetry, and its power is in its lack of abstraction. It questions itself in palpable ways — as palpable as the Urn in Keats's own hands. It questions the other poems in sensible ways — as sensible as the "leaf-fring'd legend" that haunts its shape.

That shape is haunted by young lovers — "deities or mortals"—that recall both Psyche and Cupid found in the poet's thoughtless wandering, as well as the lover feeding on his mistress's angry eyes in "Ode on Melancholy." The nightingale's song transforms into "soft pipes" that play "spirit ditties of no tone."[55] Likewise, in the "bold lover's" inability to kiss the maiden he loves we can feel Melancholy's poison that the bee-mouth sips from the flower. Most significantly, we find that the three figures who, in "Ode on Indolence," turned thrice in circles before the lazing poet have here manifested the Urn from which they seemed to magically leap into existence. Keats holds in his hand—Keats as Poet, as allegorical also himself, but also Keats as a mortal man—an art object that contains ashes and also contains some residue of all the Odes. He holds it and questions it; he turns it around in his hand and looks. And this circular activity, of both hands and mind, provides Keats with a method to ask of Poetry those questions that riddle both poet and poem with doubt.

It is the quietness of the Urn that troubles. Its silence isn't merely the silence of an object, but the silence of an object personified:

> Thou still unravish'd bride of quietness,
>   Thou foster-child of silence and slow time,
> Sylvan historian, who canst thus express
>   A flowery tale more sweetly than our rhyme:
> What leaf-fring'd legend haunts about thy shape
>   Of deities or mortals, or of both,
>   In Tempe or the dales of Arcady?
>   What men or gods are these? What maidens loth?
> What mad pursuit? What struggle to escape?
>   What pipes and timbrels? What wild ecstasy?[56]

The Urn takes its place among the long procession of brides that foster Keats's erotic imagination. She is a bride different from any other—the bride is the object of art itself. To speak of this bride, to sing of her, is to consummate a marriage Keats dearly desires: the erotic fulfillment of the loving poet to the beloved poem. But this bride resists the nuptial bed. Indeed, the Urn's very symbolic nature—despite being ringed about with images varying from gods amorously chasing "maidens loth" to the nearly orgiastic "wild ecstasy"—betrays the erotic intention of the poet. It is a container of death. Keats holds in his hand a work of art whose outward nature depicts those ceremonies—of frenzy, of music, of love, of sacrifice—that its inward nature defies. There is an empty darkness within the thing that no image can illuminate. It holds what no one can witness: the destruction of another, complete, perhaps the destruction of oneself. It is in this sense that one finds in "Ode on a Grecian Urn" a question that shakes the very faith in the art the poet practices. A poem devotedly assumes the existence of another to whom it is given—an erotic exchange of its own, the fruit of which is meaning. But this Urn holds within itself something that cannot be given. There is in the very midst of the gifted thing that which cannot be given. In the given there is the ungiveable. Keats "reads" the Urn in his hands; he also senses, discovers, that in it is that which cannot be read.

Deepening the irony is the relation of the poem Keats is writing to the object it is about. The poem does not simply describe the Urn; it makes the Urn available to be seen; it makes the Urn tangible; it is the Urn itself. "Ode on a Grecian Urn" derives much of its extraordinary power from the inherent paradox of its construction. It is the thing it attempts to describe, and its involvement with itself makes available to the poet the very agony of the art he practices.

That agony realizes that human life and the life of art are not on equal footing. The realization is not immediate. Keats

seems caught within the spell of the Urn's beauty, its de-
piction of music and love too refined to be captured by the
very human senses he has so long relied upon for his poetic
foment. He believes, or he wants to believe, that the figures
stilled into their eternal beauty play to his spirit a music it
can hear even if his mortal ears are deaf to it. The lovers
forever about to kiss live in a desire that can never be fulfilled—perhaps a small consequence to be always on the
cusp of bliss. The lovers, braided in relief on the Urn, show
back to Keats elements of his earliest poetic sensibility: the
fusion of desire and imagination in such a forceful way that,
like the sun's own energy, desire seeks not to fulfill itself,
but to extend across the whole blank chasm imagination
has opened before it. But the lovers show another aspect of
Keats's erotic epistemology he has only lately learned to see,
forced into vision as he has been by Tom's death, by his own
rattling health, by his "impossible" love for Fanny Brawne.
He sees between the "bold lover" and the beloved woman
an infinitesimal space, a gap that all eternity cannot close,
Zeno's own paradox, that silences joy's turmoil in prefer-
ence for the peace of the "cold pastoral."

We watch, as we read, Keats come to a consciousness
within the poem that he could not come to outside of the
poem—it is one of the most stunning moments in all the
poetry I know.

> Ah, happy, happy boughs! that cannot shed
>   Your leaves, nor ever bid the spring adieu;
> And, happy melodist, unwearied,
>   For ever piping songs for ever new;
> More happy love! more happy, happy love!
>   For ever warm and still to be enjoy'd,
>   For ever panting, and for ever young;
> All breathing human passion far above,
>   That leaves a heart high-sorrowful and cloy'd,
>   A burning forehead, and a parching tongue.[57]

Keats as Poet cannot help but identify with the "happy melodist." That melodist pipes as Keats in his poems sings, no world of "palpable design," but a world of "fine excess" continually new. But as he looks, as he holds the Urn and looks, two words steal into his enchantment, two words that change all. "Warm," he says. He says, "panting." These words awake in him the sensation the Urn itself had lulled him away from, and when he writes, still describing the Urn, "All breathing human passion far above," the human breathing, struggling to breathe, almost panting, hands almost fever-warm, is himself looking down at what he holds in his hands. Keats sings with a "parching tongue."

When, in the opening line of the next stanza, we read, "Who are these coming to the sacrifice?," we cannot help but suspect Keats is not among the crowd. He cannot help but see himself in position similar to the "heifer lowing at the skies, / And all her silken flanks with garlands drest." So suddenly, the fact of his mortality drops upon him. He finds himself in an unforeseeable parallel. As the sacrificial gift is led to the altar to pay heed back to the gods who govern the world, who order it, who inhale the scent of the offering with divine pleasure, so Keats has walked to the Urn he holds, likewise a kind of altar, likewise that which holds the ashes of the immolated gift.

It is as if Keats finds himself holding his own ashes in his hands. Art reminds him of his own death—a death it can show but cannot share. The deep fear in the poem is one difficult for any poet to admit, a paradox almost unfathomable. The art the poet creates does not need the poet who created it. It is for itself. Formed out of a mortal sensibility it need not heed, the Urn as figure of all Art shows in terrifying, sorrowful ways that it lives for itself, is an eternity unto itself, blissfully ignorant of the human life that formed it— of the human life it will eventually contain. Thought cannot comprehend the realization: "Thou, silent form, dost tease us out of thought / As doth eternity."[58] It is within this thoughtless gap (so sadly different than Keats's thoughtless wandering in "Ode to Psyche") that Keats hears the "silent form" speak.

> When old age shall this generation waste,
> Thou shalt remain, in midst of other woe
> Than ours, a friend to man, to whom thou say'st,
> "Beauty is truth, truth beauty,"—that is all
> Ye know on earth, and all ye need to know.[59]

That link of truth and beauty as one and the same had been since Keats's earliest creative efforts the deepest mark of his poetic faith. Now, it is as if Adam wakes from his dream to find the dream goes on dreaming itself, and does not need the sleeper's sleep to exist. The Urn speaks in silence, out of silence. Speech takes that which is internal and makes it external. It is worth considering that the words Keats hears from the Urn's mouth are spoken out of that empty blank within it, that unrepresentable space the container contains. How heartless some friendship is even in the midst of its truest kindness. The words hold within themselves an impenetrable silence. Each syllable, in its way, of "Ode on a Grecian Urn" is itself an Urn, speaking so as to preserve a silence that can be encountered in no other way. Keats speaks back. Just a line and a half. He speaks back to the Urn itself, the Urn he holds in his hands, his fevered hands, speaks with his parched tongue: "that is all / Ye know on earth, and all ye need to know." There are other things, Keats says, we've come to know.

Autumn; or, Careless on a Granary Floor

Keats walks into knowledge in autumn. Though the spring of "Ode on a Grecian Urn" will always be spring, the season around him has shifted. He writes in late September to Reynolds of the change, a description that is the germ of the great poem:

> How beautiful the season is now, how fine the air, a temperate sharpness about it. Really, without joking, chaste weather, Dian skies. I never lik'd stubble fields so much as now — Aye, better than the chilly green of the spring. Somehow a stubble plain looks warm — in the same way that some pictures look warm — this struck me so much in my [S]unday's walk that I composed upon it.[60]

Keats walks within an atmosphere divine. He treads on the mortal world, evidence of hunger and appetite present in the stubble fields. But he breathes in the immortal world. He inspires the chaste sky. For a poet who now for many years has referred to his condition as being "in a Mist," we find him suddenly in that astonishing moment when the vapors burn away. The divine air Keats walks through is also a lens of greatest clarity, and what in "To Autumn" he comes to see, he sees through an atmosphere that no longer veils his vision. He sees into what he knows.

That knowledge feels drawn from the circling despairs darkly informing the desire of "Ode on a Grecian Urn" for "more happy love." That shape, the circle, first encountered on the three figures of "Ode on Indolence" and then found again, more intimately, in Keats's own hands, as he turns the Urn around to see the entirety of its brede, offers to the poet the fundamental pattern that brings him to the bittersweet, sweet-bitter, acceptance that infuses "To Autumn." There is within "Ode on a Grecian Urn" a moment we know must exist but that we never witness. It is when the Urn has been turned one full circle, and we find ourselves again at the very beginning, where gods and mortals engage in mad pursuit and wild ecstasy. That beginning is also an end, is indecipherable from an end. Keats witnesses in the nature of the Urn's imagery, the circle of its scenes, that mythic pattern he has long inclined toward, where time ceases to be linear and is instead cyclical, returning always to the point of its own origin, finding itself, phoenix-like, always born again in the midst of its own demise. But the Urn troubles; it agonizes the very nature of the poem, the *poema*, that is, "the made thing." What we see when we read "To Autumn," when we look at the landscape through Keats's Muse-needing, Muse-haunted eyes, is the generous moment when Art reciprocates for its own possible heartlessness, when it includes within its life the lives that make it.

Keats opens the poem in ripeness so ripe it exceeds itself, a condition we must remember is also a description of the goddess the poem is dedicated to:

> Season of mists and mellow fruitfulness,
>   Close bosom-friend of the maturing sun;
> Conspiring with him how to load and bless
>   With fruit the vines that round the thatch-eves run[61]

The close-knit, nearly granular clusters of syllables that lend to the opening two lines their marked density alter after "conspiring"—here best understood as a "breathing with" as much as the more immediate connotation. The words become suddenly monosyllabic, and by the fourth line of the poem, as the iambs become so regular as to move beyond mere music into the undergirding pattern that shapes the autumnal world of the poem—as if we have now heard the unsung pattern beneath the song, the world's urgrammar—whose comforting regularity also creates an astonishing anticipation felt matched within the reader's own pulsing veins, body and poem forging their most intimate link, that as we reach the rhyme we cannot help but feel as if the fruit on the vine has burst with just the added warmth of our own attention. The poem includes us in its ripening, over-ripening concern. We know we are here witness to a scene that speaks also of our own nature, and the goddess to whom it is devoted: we find ourselves devotees. This is not a choice we make; faith isn't a choice. It is a condition.

Keats, so long a poet seeking his Muse as a reality rather than mere figure, understands the consequences of his peculiar faith — a faith that by reading Keats honestly, which is to say enthusiastically, becomes our own. He describes the nature of his religion: "I am more orthodox than to let a hethen Goddess be so neglected."[62] His orthodoxy opens him to necessary confusions. Writing to Fanny Brawne, seeking a method to (humorously) cast blessing back onto their love, he offers a heathen prayer, "if it should please Venus to hear my 'Beseech thee to hear us, O Goddess.'"[63] That prayer to Venus is also a prayer to the planet hanging in the evening sky. (Earlier in the summer, Keats wrote of both Fanny and himself staring up at night to see the comet Tralles then brightly visible.) To pray to Venus is also to devote oneself, knowingly or not, to the ambiguity inherent in the goddess-named planet; it is to pay devotional heed not only to the goddess's bright point above the earth — love as apex, love as guide — it is also to initiate oneself into a more infernal light, Lucifer's morning star, the same celestial body under a different name. Keats knows that faith is not singular, and to be devoted also requires faithfulness to what speaks itself within the prayer's intent, love's own underworld.

Helen Vendler pays keen attention to the nature of such paradoxes within "To Autumn," noting that "full-grown lambs" marks within it the impossibility of infancy and adulthood at one and the same time.[64] Such are the moments Keats's faith allows him to see; such are the mysteries into which he has become novice. Now, outside the confines of Art's "made thing," he sees in the natural world evidence of that point where death and life dovetail together and cannot be told apart. He enters that space—earthly earth and divine air—where mythic cycle and natural cycle are one and the same, where Venus and Lucifer are bound together in a bridal knot. Art shows back to us that it shares in the condition it otherwise only shows: that endless moving in life toward death, and in death, toward life.

Autumn is a Muse, is a goddess, of agriculture. "Agriculture," Keats says, "is the tamer of men."[65] Much of the beauty in "To Autumn" derives from the calmness of its acceptance, the peace inherent in its vision. Against this past spring's desire to "preserve the headlong impetuosity of my Muse,"[66] Keats has found himself in autumn tamed by the very Muse he sought to keep wild. It is a Muse reflecting back his own indolent nature.

> Who hath not seen thee oft amid thy store?
>   Sometimes whoever seeks abroad may find
> Thee sitting careless on a granary floor,
>   Thy hair soft-lifted by the winnowing wind;
> Or on a half-reap'd furrow sound asleep,
>   Drows'd with the fume of poppies, while thy hook
>   Spares the next swath and all its twined flowers:
> And sometimes like a gleaner thou dost keep
>   Steady thy laden head across a brook;
>   Or by a cyder-press, with patient look,
>   Thou watchest the last oozings hours by hours.[67]

Helen Vendler remarks that Keats makes "Autumn the voluntary agent of her own dissolution in harvest; as she winnows, so is she winnowed, her hair, the tresses of wheat, soft-lifted by the winnowing wind."[68] This goddess doesn't exempt herself from the mortal condition that opposes her own divine nature. Rather, we find her attending to her own agony — agony in the old sense, that agony Keats has been apprenticed to as a poet, the moment that has within its very creation the germ of its dissolution. It is a vision not only of universal balance, but of that "fine excess" Keats so values — though here, the point ceases to account for a poetic style as much as it does a poetic ontology. The goddess sifts through her own hair, sleeps amid the poppies of her own sickle's harvesting. Her indolence is so full of care it grows careless. That carelessness oozes out, the excessive remnant of her own genius. Her self-tending seems to say two opposite things at once: the resource is limited, but the source without end. This "hethen" faith offers Keats a poetic that empties the Urn of its ash, and lets the ash fertilize the hole into which the seeds are dropped. He sees — and the power of this vision cannot be made sophisticated, must be felt in all its simplicity — that life exceeds death. A poem — can we have such faith ourselves? — is that deathless container that, when it breaks, when the images crack, lets life spill back out. It makes auroras out of ashes. It sets the sickle inside the seed. It is there, in a love letter to Fanny Brawne, there in the excessive mistake of a single word, when in the enthusiasm of his double love, his Venus that is a Lucifer, his Lucifer that is a Venus, of loved person and poetry loved, when caught in the crisis of his two devotions, he writes of the cottages of Shanklin, on the Isle of Wight, and says they are all so romantic, covered as they are in "honeysickles."[69] The mistaken word expresses it all.

———

Or is it that the words express nothing? Can we listen through the words down into their wordless song, there where the creaturely abounds in the instinct to sing as each uniquely sings, and the veriest man among us writes so as to listen?

And full-grown lambs loud bleat from hilly bourn;
    Hedge-crickets sing; and now with treble soft
    The red-breast whistles from a garden-croft;
      And gathering swallows twitter in the skies.[70]

Here is the blatant song of the season's end, music that does not know it mourns. Here it is that in the sky the swallows gather, and find within their song what song always knows — that home is elsewhere, our most intimate home. Song introduces us to the strange fact that we do not dwell within ourselves, at least not simply so. To sing is to migrate. Song guides us away to guide us home.

Envelopes (Opened & Unopened) & Aeolian Harps

In August 1820, Keats has begun to waste away, though to look at him one might not know it. He might seem only fevered, mind strung at too high a pitch. But invisible to the eye, inwardly, within the body, the lungs become—day by day—their brittle parchment. He is staying at Leigh Hunt's, in the chaotic whirl of the house on Mortimer Terrace. Keats has been waiting for a reply from a letter he wrote to Fanny Brawne: "Every hour I am more and more concentrated in you. Everything else tastes like chaff in my Mouth."[1] Fanny's response had come two days earlier, but Keats wasn't given the letter. A maid had opened it, perhaps read it. In a fury, in a fever, Keats leaves—but has no home to return to, has no money, is bereft. He wanders through Hampstead. The door he ends up knocking on is at Wentworth Place; the door is the Brawnes'. Mrs. Brawne opens the door; Keats sick, poor Keats—she lets him in.

I like to think of Keats right then, in fever of body and fever of mind, disheveled, penniless, desperately in love and desperate in desperation itself. I like to think of that moment when being outside the house of the young woman he loves becomes the moment when the inner and the outer no longer hold their opposition, when the door opens, and the tenuous boundary becomes generous. I like to see as Mrs. Brawne must have seen, opening the door so suddenly. A male figure, short, slumped or leaning, or standing back as if expecting to be shunned, or about to turn away, but darkened, a silhouette, no features visible. And I like to think of Mrs. Brawne's eye adjusting itself to the outer light, and the slow revelation that the featureless face is Keats's own.

Gertrude Stein says of herself through Alice B. Toklas's mouth: "She always was, she always is, tormented by the problem of the external and the internal."[2]

Let us say that the poet's condition is one tormented by externals and internals. There is a page-thin line that divides one from the other; there is a wooden door that marks the difference; a parchment, a vellum, this very skin; there is the eye looking outward as the world pours in, the mind dreaming behind the eye's gaze, "half-creating" what of the world it sees.

There is a handwritten word that contains in it the heart's dearest utterance, a page folded over upon itself and sealed in an envelope. The letter—it is its own lovely torment, mimicking as it does the lover's own crisis, outer and inner, expression and thought, body and soul. The intimacy of opening a letter, of tearing open the envelope, of unfolding the page, of finding there in dark words of the woman whom you love yourself addressed and no one else; words her own hand marked, words carrying her own breath as she moved her lips to the words she wrote, speaking so quietly she cannot hear herself. Keats could kiss her hand by kissing the page. Keats would sleep with her letter under his pillow; once he awoke to find the waxen seal missing.

A letter is an erotic omen.

Parallels terrify, then grow luminous.

The inner life contained in the outer form—a problem poetic, personal, biological. The poet might do all he can to keep within himself the unfolding beauties wandering of themselves through his mind, inviting him into himself as one might walk into a bower. Love says "enter" and shows the lover a secret door. The poet goes in to walk out, tries to solve the Gordian knot of self and self-perception not by cutting the knot in two, but by turning it inside out. Poetry is a threshold art; every threshold is Eros's difficult test.

In Italy, before the crisis grows undeniably mortal, Keats sees Canova's statue of the nude Princess Borghese and renames it the "Aeolian Harp." The nude reclines in the marble just as the nude reclines in the mind. Breath blows across the body and there is the song. Thought, the poet doesn't forget, is a breathy thing, and wind just the wingburst of Eros's strident flight.

Dying in Rome, Severn by his side, Keats refuses to open any letters. His nerves cannot bear the sound of Fanny's name. He wants to be buried with her letters, to have them wound into his winding cloth.

When Keats dies, the doctor performing the autopsy finds the lungs to be entirely destroyed.

The grave is a letter that cannot be opened once it is sealed. Keats was buried with Fanny's unopened letters— there in the earth's very dark, no one could open again those envelopes meant for no one's eyes, not even his own.

Some few weeks later, Severn notes, after visiting Keats's grave, that "now he lies at rest with the flowers he so desired above him."[3] The daisies grow out from the grave ground. I rename them myself: Aeolian Harp. Listen—. Listen as Keats knew to listen. Listen so as to see. There's Keats's face, sung by the wind through the flowers winding.

1820

The Many Last Months:
Imagination's Ambivalence

On 6 February Keats writes a letter to his little sister Fanny
giving the cause of the serious downturn in his health:
"From imprudently leaving off my great coat in the thaw
I caught a cold which flew to my Lungs."[1] What he does
not say is that, after riding home on the outside of a carriage through weather quite suddenly turned awful — thaw
returning to the season's freeze — he walked into the quarters he shared with Charles Brown and hemorrhaged blood
from his mouth. So began many months of convalescence,
set back always by another spitting of blood, often occurring
at the point when Keats felt he might finally recover. Or so
he said in his letters, when he could muster a bright mood in
which to write — that he might recover. He knew that spitting of blood on 3 February was his "death-warrant."[2]

Death did not come quick. Death is over a year away.
Death is in another country. But Keats knows, as if inscribed
within himself, as if his mind is reading over and again the
heart's insistent sentence, that he is dying, and that every
possibility he cherished in his life — from fame to his love
for Fanny Brawne — has become impossible. "I cannot say
forget me," he writes to Fanny in one of his nearly daily letters, "but I would mention that there are impossibilities in
the world."[3]

Aristotle makes a bewildering and beautiful claim about
the sensibility of the great poet in comparison to a lesser:
"Things probable though impossible should be preferred
to the possible but improbable."[4] One of the measures of
Keats's greatness can be felt, seen, heard, in the ways in
which he shows that our perceptive lives forge those links
that trace the vertiginous path of probable impossibilities.

Sensation reveals the actuality of probable impossibilities in ways that thought often shuns; sensation isn't bound to those "consequitive reasonings"[5] of which Keats is so critical, connections a mere logic insists upon, those seemingly sound improbable possibilities. A probable impossibility insists on the poem's ability to enter into those realms the poem itself has opened, and doesn't hem back at the impossible vision seen only from the impossible vantage point. Keats leaps over those chasms imagination opens, leaps into them — chasms imagination must also fill.

Declining Shelley's offer to have Keats stay with him in Italy, Keats offers this writing advice:

> *An artist* must serve Mammon; he must have 'self-concentration,' selfishness perhaps. You, I am sure, will forgive me for sincerely remarking that you might curb your magnanimity and be more of an artist, and 'load every rift' of your subject with ore.[6]

The advice says much of the poet Keats found himself to be — or, now that he is so firmly within the process of ceasing to be, the poet he knows he would have become. Keats wants a poem to be that which fills itself with source; he wants not the golden artifact, but the gold. It is a strange vision for what a poem might offer, for it undoes the assumed end of the work of art as a finished thing, ornate in beauty, whose pleasure comes in appreciating what another has done (which is often to say, what I cannot do myself). Keats's aesthetic vision differs. He wants a poem to include within it those rifts and chasms that well might tear the poem and its world apart. But it is within those rifts, those ruptures that probable impossibilities inflict on the poem that contains them, that the reader finds the ore by which to create not an appreciation of the poem in hand, but an ore to forge another poem. This writing work, Keats says, is elemental. It is where Mammon's idol is melted back down into ore.

Keats is not forging other poems, not really, not now. That ore is for others, buried resplendent in his work, shining sun-diamonds on a swift-moving stream, but hidden from his own eyes. He feels much more — as his nerves torment him into the continual realization of his own death — that he has failed as a poet.

> Now I have had opportunities of passing nights anxious and awake I have found other thoughts intrude upon me. 'If I should die,' said I to myself, 'I have left no immortal work behind me, nothing to make my friends proud of my memory, but I have lov'd the principle of beauty in all things, and if I had time I would have made myself remember'd.[7]

To "love the principle of Beauty" may well be to love a principle impossibly unprincipled, for beauty is still that which "obliterates consideration" in favor of more palpable becomings, obedient to a logic of the world and not a logical idea of the world — as a leaf becomes the tree's logical proof of the nightly questionable sun.

What has shifted in Keats since the close of the great Odes, since abandoning the mythico-lyric beauty of *The Fall of Hyperion: A Dream* is not the naked fact of his mortality, but the way in which he lives within the probable impossibility of his own death: "I have an habitual feeling of my real life having past, and that I am leading a posthumous existence."[8] Keats has entered into the realm his poems alone ventured into before, the realm his poems made available to him, this work of imagination. That realm is one between this world and another, between life and death, and the poem offers an impossible ground on which those contraries can coexist. It is nervy work: audacious, yes; but also formed by the very senses the poem must be able to evoke in a reader. Keats's fevered life has thrust him bodily into a poetic condition, perhaps the very condition of his own poetics. He is and is not. No longer Aristotle's genius able to write into being those probable impossibilities that bloom in the bowers of his poems, he finds himself having become a probable impossibility. He has the feel of it in him, his posthumous living. He isn't alive *or* dead, but alive *and* dead, witness to what cannot be witnessed, experiencing what refuses all experience. He cannot find a way to speak of it, for it is unspeakable. He has found that terrible ground perhaps Art alone makes accessible in ways that can be endured. But here there is no enduring; it is not Art, dying. Keats lives in the placeless place of his own death. A poem can survive it. A man can't. He can't survive it even as he is alive within it. No one witnesses the witness.

Keats exists in nervous ambivalence. At times, when he hopes he might recover, he returns to a sensibility that might again make writing a line of poetry possible:

> I may say that for 6 Months before I was taken ill I had not passed a tranquil day, either that gloom overspread me or I was suffering under some passionate feeling, or if I turn'd to versify that acerbated the poison of either sensation. The Beauties of Nature had lost their power over me. How astonishingly (here I must premise that illness as far as I can judge in so short a time has relieved my Mind of a load of deceptive thoughts and images and makes me perceive things in a truer light), how astonishingly does the chance of leaving the world impress a sense of its natural beauties on us. Like poor Falstaff, though I do not babble, I think of green fields. I muse with the greatest affection on every flower I have known from my infancy. Their shapes and colours are as new to me as if I had just created them with a superhuman fancy. It is because they are connected with the most thoughtless and happiest moments of our Lives. I have seen foreign flowers in hothouses of the most beautiful nature,

but I do not care a straw for them. The simple flowers of
our spring are what I want to see again.[9]

He reiterates the same notion to Fanny Brawne, though
with an added darkness: "I see everything over again eternally that I ever have seen. If I get on the pleasant clue I live
in a sort of happy misery, if on the unpleasant 'tis a miserable
misery."[10] His posthumous life returns him to a sort of Arcadia, where the flowers need no names to be known. Often,
though, his mood turns away from his "happy misery," and
he suffers less redeemable agonies.

Imagination had long been Keats's crucible for agonistic
work. Now Keats blames his imagination for the agony he
suffers. He is "convinc'd I shall die of agony."[11] That agony
is rooted in his imagination always opening before him that
which he knows cannot occur.

> There is one thought enough to kill me. I have been well,
> healthy, alert, etc., walking with her, and now the knowl-
> edge of contrast, feeling for light and shade, all that infor-
> mation (primitive sense) necessary for a poem are great
> enemies to the recovery of the stomach.[12]

Doctors and friends concur: the stretch of his imagination
over many years is what is killing him. "The Doctor assures
me that there is nothing the matter with me except nervous irritability and a general weakness of the whole system which has proceeded from my anxiety of mind of late
years and the too great excitement of poetry."[13] He is told
the Muse he sought is killing him; he believes it himself.
"Who are these coming to the sacrifice?" As true as it might
have been in years past to speak of the imagination in connection to Keats's magnetic erotics, imagination now seems
to magnify more than magnetize. Writing of Fanny Brawne
to Charles Brown: "I eternally see her figure eternally van-
ishing."[14] Writing to his sister: "I am too nervous to enter
into any discussion in which my heart is concerned."[15] Of

Brawne to Brown, again: "To see her handwriting would break my heart."[16] (To love Keats is to believe he is not exaggerating.) Again, to Brown: "I am so weak (in mind) that I cannot bear the sight of any handwriting of a friend I love so much as I do you."[17]

To this poet, to this man Keats, for whom person and place pressed upon him until he became other than himself; to this man of no self, no character, to this man all poet, all perception, now his imagination brings that which pressing into him would break him apart. He is cast on the shoals of himself. Himself is what is breaking himself apart—ocean and rock and ship all one and all at once. How shocking it is to know that in writing from Naples to Fanny Brawne's mother, this poet of all-feel now says, "I do not feel in this world."[18] How heartbreaking to know the heart is a thing that can break. We know it is so when we read that this poet of half-light, of dwelling in uncertainty, of refusing the ease of fact and reason against mystery's needed irritations, can no longer exist in "agonies and uncertainties."[19] His fever has worn him out.

> Thou art a dreaming thing;
> A fever of thyself—[20]

I wonder if to read Keats is also to become contagious oneself. Is his fever mine? This is a question a poet must ask when reading Keats. Is his fever mine? Who does not grow flush as words darken the blank page? Ink has a quick feel; it feels as if it quickens the heart. (Right now, as I type these last sentences, I hear the breeze blow through the apple tree. It sounds like a brook. And so, dreaming thing, I think of green fields.) I think of green fields, and in that green field, I see an impossible thing. Keats writes his last letter to Brown; he knows it will be his last. "I can scarcely bid you good bye even in a letter. I always made an awkward bow."[21] There in the green field I see Keats eternally making his awkward bow.

The Late Flowers

Brown writes to William Haslam, 3 December 1820: "Yet the spitting of blood is a fact."[1]

The word *poem* and the word *fact* share an etymological base. Both derive from "the made thing."

The word *blood* and the word *blossom* share a root in *bhel*: to thrive, bloom, blow, sprout.

The fact of blood is that it unfolds from the mouth, as does a poem.

Keats and Severn sailed to Naples, but Keats wanted to die in Rome.

Severn hired them a carriage, and they rode through the still blossoming fields. They left on 31 October 1820, and the flowers to Keats must have seemed living past their rightful bounds. Severn was so deeply struck by the beauty of the wildflowers that he couldn't stay cooped up in the carriage with his dying friend. He stepped out and walked beside as Keats rode within, "& as the carriage went slow enough I got down & walked nearly the whole way & delighted Keats by gathering the wild flowers."[2] Severn threw the gathered buds through the carriage's open window, and as the miles took them closer to Rome, the wildflowers gathered around Keats, burying him in petals and scent.

At the bottom of the public stairs Keats stared out at from his room is a statue of a sinking ship.

When Keats seemed in recovering health, Severn would go out. He returned one day carrying roses, ebullient at finding them blooming when in England the roses all would be dormant.

Keats saw the roses and wept.

Flowers were for him, he said, always a refuge in which he could forget the difficulty of world and life and luxuriate in beauty alone. He said he had hoped to die before spring would allow him to see roses again.[3]

———

Four days before Keats's death Severn held him so tremblingly that Keats tried to calm him for fear of being too convulsed as he died in his friend's arms. "[H]e said, 'did you ever see anyone die' no — 'well then I pity you poor Severn — what trouble and danger you have got into for me — now you must be firm for it will not last long — I shall soon be laid in the quiet grave — thank God for the quiet grave — O! I can feel the cold earth upon me — the daisies growing over me — O for this quiet — it will be my first' — "[4]

Dr. Clark, who attended Keats in Rome with tremendous, if sometimes misguided, care, joined the few people present at Keats's burial. "The good hearted Doctor made the men put tufts of daisies upon the grave — he said — 'this would be poor Keats's wish — could he know it' — ."[5]

In May Severn went to visit the cemetery: "[B]ut now thank God it is all quit and over — poor Keats has his wish — a humble wish indeed — he is at peace in the quiet grave — I walked there a few days ago and found the daisies grown all over it — "[6]

Of His Hand

Soon after his death, many of Keats's dearest friends attempted to write down his life. All of them failed in completing their projects, as if the fragmentary nature of Keats's history refused completion even when transferred to another's still living hands. Severn, Keats's friend and nurse and confidant through his last, wasting days, didn't put pen to paper immediately — save for his letters recording those heartrending last days — but instead put paint to canvas. The paintings he produced bear the mark of Severn's need to paint Keats in the most "poetic" light, giving us not the poet embroiled in the very crisis of what it means to write a poem, not the poet in his pugilistic pride and the difficulty of imaginative rapture, but the poet as pale, inspired flower, whose gift is too rare to survive this troubled, troubling world.

I find it strange to realize that in Keats's greatest ode, "To Autumn," unlike the other Odes, the poet as speaking subject hardly exists. So deeply ingrained is the poem in its perceptive life that saying "I" would falsely limit the nature of the vision whose imaginative force expands past the self's mere limit. Keats has himself disappeared into the poem.

But when the poet disappears in life his friends deny him the absence he so longed for. His hope for an anonymous tomb is ignored in spirit if upheld in letter. He is, as it were, being ceaselessly dragged back into the identity from whose grasp he had finally slipped away.

George Keats, writing to Dilke some eleven years after his brother's death, says: "Do you hear anything of Severn, I am anxious to have some *painting* of his, for which I desire to pay *well*, he was kind to John, and is the last link of association in my mind with John and life—could you put me in the way of obtaining *one*, what are his circumstances—..."[1] The image of life fills in the place of the life itself, that life gone missing, past the threshold of any living grasp.

Severn began one painting of Keats—one of the most well known—almost immediately after Keats's death. Indeed, he claimed to John Taylor that in May of 1821 it was already almost done: "I am very happy at what you tell me about your intended memoir of Keats—his bea[u]tiful character will astonish people—for very few knew it.— I will make every communication to you—but not yet— I cannot stand it—only writing this has made me like a child.—I have begun a small whole length of him—from last seeing him at Hampstead—this I will finish and send to you—..."[2] In the painting Keats is sitting cross-legged in a chair, one arm leaning against another chair, his hand holding up his head that is bent down to the open book in his lap. The light in the painting comes through the open window, a thick, sentimental light. Keats's other hand holds open the book at its binding, its odd weight on the recto page, his eyes gazing down on the verso. His angelic aura speaks lovingly, but falsely.

In the letter in which Severn describes Keats's death, he mentions a seemingly insignificant fact: "On the following day a cast was taken—and his death made known to the brutes here . . ."[3] Casts were taken not only of Keats's face, but of his hand and foot. Taylor would like them sent to him, but Severn is still in need of their presence: "The casts I must send another time—because I shall require them to finish the picture from . . ."[4]

The picture Severn speaks of is the portrait of Keats reading in Hampstead. The ease of the portrait is meant to catch Keats in a habitual stance, reading by the open window, the verdure outside matched only by the imaginative verdure invisible within the poet himself. His hand holds down the book — and as one looks at that hand, it seems to hold down the book with a weight far beyond the needed pressure, a weight that seems like it could push through the page, push through the book, sever itself from the poet's arm, and crash awfully to the ground. It looks like the hand of a dead man. That hand rests on a book resting in Keats's lap in the center of the painting, and it becomes the visual point around which the whole portrait depends. It is a point not unlike Euclid's definition: "A point is that which has no part." For Keats's hand here is a dead hand, and has no part with the painter's effort to present him as if in life once again. It contains in itself a deathly weight the painting cannot alter.

It is this dead hand that holds the book down.

One of the last poems John Keats wrote makes of himself a ghost before he has died:

> This living hand, now warm and capable
> Of earnest grasping, would, if it were cold
> And in the icy silence of the tomb,
> So haunt thy days and chill thy dreaming nights
> That thou would wish thine own heart dry of blood,
> So in my veins red life might stream again,
> And thou be conscience-calm'd. See, here it is —
> I hold it towards you.[5]

In ghastly echo of the Urn's "Who are these coming to the sacrifice?" — and that line's heart-wrenching realization that the poet himself is one that is coming, is that one who is perhaps himself the sacrifice — Keats writes a poem that demands the reader's own sacrificial response. It is a chilling force that demands "That thou would wish thine own heart dry of blood, / So in my veins red life might stream again," reminiscent of the oldest sacrificial rites, the rites of Aversion, where blood was given back to those chthonic gods whose bloodless hearts craved only blood to live again, and so appease their fury, and avert their harm.

The "living hand" of the poem's first line has become, by the last line, a hand either living or dead, perhaps living *and* dead. The poem accuses us who read it of being at fault in such a way that the only calm our conscience can find would be in exchanging our own life for the poet's. Unlike Lady Macbeth's hand that cannot cease in bearing the evidence of her guilt, this hand cannot cease in accusing us of ours — not our own blood-stained hand, but our hand coursing with blood within it, pulse-full, vital, holding the page on which the poem is printed. The work of the poet's hand is the poem itself, a metonymy that makes of any group of lines a haunted realm where to read the poem as livingly as it was written is not to come to any understanding of meaning, but is to grasp the poem in such a way that found within it is the poet's own hand, warm and capable once again. The page is so often nothing more than an "icy tomb." But then the reader's eye can be a little sun. Then the tomb's ice thaws and becomes the flowering field. And the hand buried there finds blood in its veins again, and climbs through itself back into life. "See, here it is — / I hold it towards you."

I keep trying to imagine how that hand is held towards me. Sometimes it is with index finger pointing directly at me, finding in me some guilt I did not know was mine to feel. Other times, the hand is open, a gesture of gratitude, thanking me for some gift I did not know I could bestow. Sometimes it is open as if to beckon me in. Reading seems to become a form of death and a form of life, both opposites simultaneously. To read Keats's poem is to suffer a small portion of his death, one finely attuned to the fact of our own mortality; to read the poem is to lend back to its words a portion of our own life, one astonishingly aware that any immortality is composed of our own eye's brief flicker, and that recognition found deep in the blood as it surges toward the heart and away, that this pulse in human life may best be called thought.

NOTES

Apology

1. Stanley Plumly's *Posthumous Keats: A Personal Biography* (New York: Norton, 2008) contains a wonderful analysis of images of Keats in the chapter "On He Flared."
2. Keats. Letter to George and Tom Keats, 15 April 1817. *Selected Letters of John Keats.* Ed. Grant F. Scott. Rev. ed. Cambridge: Harvard U P, 2002. All letters by Keats are from this collection and are henceforth cited by recipient and date only. Question marks indicate uncertainty as to the specific date.
3. Keats. "To Charles Cowden Clarke." *Complete Poems.* Ed. Jack Stillinger. Cambridge: Belknap P of Harvard U P, 1982. All poems by Keats are from this collection and are henceforth cited by title only.
4. Please see Robert Gittings, "Keats's Debt to Dante," *The Mask of Keats* (Cambridge: Harvard U P, 1956), for further thoughts on the deep influence of Dante on Keats's work and thinking.
5. Keats. *Hyperion.*
6. Ibid.

A Note on the Book

1. Keats. Letter to J. H. Reynolds, 19 February 1818.
2. Duncan, Robert. *The H.D. Book.* Berkeley: U of California P, 2010.
3. Ibid.

First Portrait: Young Keats, Weeping Beneath the Desk

1. Clarke, Charles Cowden. "Recollections of John Keats." *Rare Early Essays on John Keats.* Ed. Carmen Joseph Della Buono. Darby, PA: Norwood, 1980.

1816

1. Hesiod. *Theogony.* Trans. Apostolos N. Athanassakis. Baltimore: Johns Hopkins U P, 1983.
2. Keats. "Fill for me a brimming bowl."
3. Keats. Letter to C. C. Clarke, 9 October 1816.
4. Keats. "To Charles Cowden Clarke."
5. Ibid.
6. Ibid.

7. Keats. "Sleep and Poetry."

8. Keats. "To My Brother George." Sonnet.

9. Keats. "To My Brother George." Epistle.

10. Keats. Letter to John Taylor, 27 February 1818.

11. Keats. "On First Looking into Chapman's Homer."

12. Ibid.

13. Davenport, Guy, trans. "Herakleitos." *Seven Greeks*. New York: New Directions, 1995.

14. Keats. Letter to J. H. Reynolds, 17, 18 April 1817.

15. Keats. "How many bards gild the lapses of time."

16. Keats. "To G. A. W."

17. Keats. "Sleep and Poetry."

18. Ibid.

19. Ibid.

20. Ibid.

21. Ibid.

22. Keats. "To one who has been long in city pent."

23. Ibid.

24. Keats. "To a Friend Who Sent Me Some Roses."

25. Keats. "Calidore: A Fragment."

26. Keats. "O Solitude! if I must with thee dwell."

27. Ibid.

28. Keats. "Woman! when I behold thee flippant, vain."

29. Ibid.

30. Blake, William. "The Grey Monk." *The Selected Poems of William Blake*. Hertfordshire: Wordsworth, 1994.

31. Pound, Ezra. "A Few Don'ts." *Poetry Magazine*. March 1913.

32. Ibid.

33. Keats. "I stood tip-toe upon a little hill."

34. Keats. "To Autumn."

35. Keats. "I stood tip-toe upon a little hill."

Second Portrait: Apprenticeship

1. Clarke, Charles Cowden. "Recollections of John Keats." *Rare Early Essays on John Keats*. Ed. Carmen Joseph Dello Buono. Darby, PA: Norwood, 1980.

2. Ibid.

3. Agamben, Giorgio. "Melencholia I." *Stanzas: Word and Phantasm in Western Culture*. Trans. Ronald L. Martinez. Minneapolis: U of Minnesota P, 1993.

4. Agamben, Giorgio. *"Spiritus phantasticus."* Ibid.

5. Agamben, Giorgio. "Narcissus and Pygmalion." Ibid.

6. Rollins, Hyder Edward, ed. *The Keats Circle*. Vol. 1. Cambridge: Harvard U P, 1965.

7. Rollins, Hyder Edward, ed. *The Keats Circle*. Vol. 2. Cambridge: Harvard U P, 1965.

1817

1. Ward, Aileen. *John Keats: The Making of a Poet*. Rev. ed. New York: Farrar, 1986.

2. Keats. Letter to J. H. Reynolds, 17, 18 April 1817.

3. Keats. "To a Young Lady Who Sent Me a Laurel Crown."

4. Keats. "On Receiving a Laurel Crown from Leigh Hunt."

5. Keats. "God of the golden bow."

6. Ibid.

7. Keats. Letter to B. R. Haydon, 10, 11 May 1817.

8. Ibid. For more on Keats and the notion of genius Haydon introduced him to, see Patterson, Charles. *The Daemonic in the Poetry of John Keats*. Urbana: U of Illinois P, 1970.

9. Ibid.

10. Keats. Letter to Benjamin Bailey, 8 October 1817.

11. Keats. *Endymion*.

12. Ibid.

13. Ibid.

14. Keats. Letter to Benjamin Bailey, 22 November 1817.

15. Jones, James Land. *Adam's Dream: Mythic Consciousness in Keats and Yeats*. Athens: U of Georgia P, 1975.

16. Keats. Letter to George and Tom Keats, 21, 27 (?) December 1817.

17. Emerson, Ralph Waldo. "The Poet." *Emerson's Essays*. New York: Perennial, 1926.

18. Celan, Paul. "Bremen Prize Acceptance Speech." *Selected Poems and Prose of Paul Celan*. Trans. John Felstiner. New York: Norton, 2001.

19. Keats. *Endymion*.

20. Ibid.

21. Ibid.

22. Ibid.

23. Wordsworth, William. "Tintern Abbey." *Wordsworth and Coleridge: Lyrical Ballads 1798*. Ed. W. J. B. Owen. 2nd ed. Oxford: Oxford U P, 1983.

24. Eliade, Mircea. *The Sacred and the Profane*. Trans. Willard R. Trask. New York: Harcourt, 1957.

25. Keats. *Endymion*.
26. Thomas, Dylan. *Selected Poems 1914–1953*. New York: New Directions, 1956.
27. Agamben, Giorgio. "Genius." *Profanations*. Trans. Jeff Fork. New York: Zone Books, 2007.
28. Ibid.
29. Keats. *Endymion*.
30. Keats. Letter to Benjamin Bailey, 22 November 1817.
31. Ibid.
32. Ibid.
33. Keats. Letter to George and Tom Keats, 21, 27 (?) December 1817.

Third Portrait: Ascent & Descent

1. Plumly, Stanley. *Posthumous Keats: A Personal Biography*. New York: Norton, 2008.
2. Gittings, Robert. "Keats's Debt to Dante." *The Mask of Keats*. Cambridge: Harvard U P, 1956. The essay is also very helpful in documenting Dante's influence on the first *Hyperion*.
3. Keats. "Read me a lesson, Muse, and speak it loud."
4. Keats. Letter to Tom Keats, 23, 26 July 1818.

1818

1. Keats. Letter to J. A. Hessey, 26 October 1818.
2. Ibid.
3. Keats. Letter to John Taylor, 27 February 1818.
4. Keats. Letter to Richard Woodhouse, 27 October 1818.
5. Keats. Letter to John Taylor, 27 February 1818.
6. Keats. Letter to George and Georgiana Keats, 14–31 October 1818.
7. Keats. Letter to George and Tom Keats, 21 February 1818.
8. Keats. Letter to J. H. Reynolds, 3 February 1818.
9. Keats. Letter to Benjamin Bailey, 23 January 1818.
10. Keats. "Lines on Seeing a Lock of Milton's Hair."
11. Keats. Letter to B. R. Haydon, 8 April 1818.
12. Keats. Letter to George and Tom Keats, 23, 24 January 1818.
13. Keats. Letter to J. H. Reynolds, 19 February 1818.
14. Ibid.
15. Ibid.
16. Keats. "When I have fears that I may cease to be."
17. Keats. Letter to John Taylor, 27 February 1818.
18. Keats. Letter to Benjamin Bailey, 23 January 1818.

19. Keats. Letter to J. H. Reynolds, 19 February 1818.

20. Keats. Letter to J. H. Reynolds, 3 May 1818.

21. Keats. Letter to John Taylor, 30 January 1818.

22. Keats. "Fancy."

23. Keats. "In drear nighted December."

24. Keats. Letter to J. H. Reynolds, 3 May 1818.

25. Keats. Letter to Tom Keats, 25–27 June 1818.

26. Keats. Letter to Benjamin Bailey, 18, 22 July 1818.

27. Keats. Letter to Tom Keats, 3, 6 August 1818.

28. Keats. "Read me a lesson, Muse, and speak it loud."

29. Keats. Letter to C. W. Dilke, 20, 21 September 1818.

30. Agamben, Giorgio. *Remnants of Auschwitz*. Trans. Daniel Heller-Roazen. New York: Zone Books, 2002. Agamben's examination of the "musselmann" of Auschwitz relies on Primo Levi's account, which described the most starved, most depleted prisoners as those who have "seen the Gorgon." The book is unexpectedly helpful in considering the deeper issues of witness, and Keats's own relation to expression and the realization of death (his own and others).

31. Keats. Letter to J. H. Reynolds, 22 (?) September 1818.

32. Keats. Letter to George and Georgiana Keats, 14–31 October 1818.

33. Keats. *Endymion*.

34. Keats. "On First Looking into Chapman's Homer."

35. Keats. "Dear Reynolds, as last night I lay in bed."

36. Keats. "God of the meridian."

37. Keats. Letter to John Taylor, 30 January 1818.

38. Keats. Letter to Benjamin Bailey, 13 March 1818.

39. Keats. Letter to James Rice, 24 March 1818.

40. Keats. Letter to J. H. Reynolds, 14 March 1818.

41. Keats. Letter to George and Georgiana Keats, 14–31 October 1818.

Fourth Portrait: Of Thrushes & Sparrows
(A Palimpsest, 1817–1820)

1. Keats. Letter to Benjamin Bailey, 22 November 1817.

2. Keats. Letter to J. H. Reynolds, 19 February 1818.

3. Keats. "Dear Reynolds, as last night I lay in bed."

4. Brown, Charles. "Life of John Keats." Ed. Hyder Edward Rollins. *The Keats Circle*. Vol. 2. Cambridge: Harvard U P, 1965.

5. Keats. Letter to Fanny Brawne, 24 (?) February 1820.

6. Keats. Letter to Fanny Brawne, 1 March (?) 1820.

7. Keats. Letter to Fanny Brawne, March (?) 1820.

8. Keats. Letter to Fanny Brawne, February (?) 1820.

9. Keats. Letter to Fanny Brawne, March (?) 1820.

1819

1. Keats. Letter to Miss Jeffrey, 31 May 1819.

2. Keats. Letter to Charles Brown, 23 September 1819.

3. Ibid.

4. Keats. *The Fall of Hyperion: A Dream*.

5. Keats. Letter to George and Georgiana Keats, 17–27 September 1819.

6. Keats. Letter to Fanny Brawne, 16 August 1819.

7. Keats. Letter to George and Georgiana Keats, 17–27 September 1819.

8. Keats. Letter to Fanny Brawne, 13 October 1819.

9. Keats. Letter to Benjamin Bailey, 16 August 1819.

10. Hawhee, Deborah. *Bodily Arts: Rhetoric and Athletics in Ancient Greece.* Austin: U of Texas P, 2004.

11. Keats. Letter to Fanny Keats, 12 April 1819.

12. Keats. Letter to Benjamin Bailey, 23 January 1818.

13. Keats. Letter to B. R. Haydon, 13 April 1819.

14. Keats. Letter to B. R. Haydon, 8 March 1819.

15. Keats. Letter to George and Georgiana Keats, 14 February–4 May 1819.

16. Ibid.

17. Keats. "Ode on Indolence."

18. Ibid.

19. Ibid.

20. Ibid.

21. Ibid.

22. Ibid.

23. Keats. "Ode to Psyche."

24. Ibid.

25. Ibid.

26. Keats. Letter to George and Georgiana Keats, 14 February–4 May 1819.

27. Ibid.

28. Keats. "Ode to Psyche."

29. Ibid.

30. Ibid.

31. Keats. "Ode on Melancholy."

32. Ibid.

33. Keats. Letter to George and Georgiana Keats, 14 February–4 May 1819.

34. Ibid.

35. Keats. Letter to Fanny Brawne, 16 August 1819.

36. Keats. Letter to Fanny Brawne, 5, 6 August 1819.

37. Keats. Letter to Fanny Brawne, 25 July 1819.

38. Keats. "Ode on Melancholy."

39. Ibid.

40. Ibid.

41. Keats. Letter to George and Georgiana Keats, 14 February–4 May 1819.

42. Keats. Letter to Fanny Brawne, 15 July 1819.

43. Keats. "Ode on Melancholy."

44. Keats. "Dear Reynolds, as last night I lay in bed."

45. Keats. "Ode to a Nightingale."

46. Keats. Letter to George and Georgiana Keats, 14 February–4 May 1819.

47. Keats. "Ode to a Nightingale."

48. Keats. Letter to Richard Woodhouse, 27 October 1818.

49. Keats. Letter to J. H. Reynolds, 11 July 1819.

50. Keats. "Ode to a Nightingale."

51. Ibid.

52. Ibid.

53. Keats. *Hyperion.*

54. Keats. "Ode to a Nightingale."

55. Keats. "Ode on a Grecian Urn."

56. Ibid.

57. Ibid.

58. Ibid.

59. Ibid.

60. Keats. Letter to J. H. Reynolds, 21 September 1819.

61. Keats. "To Autumn."

62. Keats. Letter to George and Georgiana Keats, 14 February–4 May 1819.

63. Keats. Letter to Fanny Brawne, 5, 6 August 1819.

64. Vendler, Helen. *The Odes of John Keats.* Cambridge: Belknap P of Harvard U P, 1983.

65. Keats. Letter to John Taylor, 5 September 1819.

66. Keats. Letter to George and Georgiana Keats, 14 February–May 4 1819.

67. Keats. "To Autumn."

68. Vendler, Helen. *The Odes of John Keats.* Cambridge: Belknap P of Harvard U P, 1983.

69. Keats. Letter to Fanny Keats, 6 July 1819.

70. Keats. "To Autumn."

Fifth Portrait: Envelopes (Opened & Unopened) & Aeolian Harps

1. Keats. Letter to Fanny Brawne, August (?) 1820.
2. Stein, Gertrude. *The Autobiography of Alice B. Toklas*. New York: Quality Paperback Book Club, 1993.
3. Severn, Joseph. Letter to William Haslam, 5 May 1821. *Selected Letters of John Keats*. Ed. Grant F. Scott. Rev. ed. Cambridge: Harvard U P, 2002.

1820

1. Keats. Letter to Fanny Keats, 6 February 1820.
2. Quoted in *Selected Letters of John Keats*, from Charles Brown's "Life of John Keats."
3. Keats. Letter to Fanny Brawne, February (?) 1820.
4. Aristotle. *The Poetics*. Trans. Stephen Halliwell. Cambridge: Harvard U P, 1995. Loeb Classical Library.
5. Keats. Letter to Benjamin Bailey, 22 November 1817.
6. Keats. Letter to Percy Bysshe Shelley, 16 August 1820.
7. Keats. Letter to Fanny Brawne, February (?) 1820.
8. Keats. Letter to Charles Brown, 30 November 1820.
9. Keats. Letter to James Rice, 14, 16 February 1820.
10. Keats. Letter to Fanny Brawne, June (?) 1820.
11. Keats. Letter to Fanny Brawne, May (?) 1820.
12. Keats. Letter to Charles Brown, 30 November 1820.
13. Keats. Letter to Fanny Keats, 21 April 1820.
14. Keats. Letter to Charles Brown, 30 September 1820.
15. Keats. Letter to Fanny Keats, 12 April 1820.
16. Keats. Letter to Charles Brown, 1, 2 November 1820.
17. Keats. Letter to Charles Brown, 30 November 1820.
18. Keats. Letter to Mrs. Samuel Brawne, 24 (?) October 1820.
19. Keats. Letter to Fanny Brawne, May (?) 1820.
20. Keats. *The Fall of Hyperion: A Dream*.
21. Keats. Letter to Charles Brown, 30 November 1820.

Sixth Portrait: The Late Flowers

1. Rollins, Hyder Edward, ed. *The Keats Circle*. Vol. 2. Cambridge: Harvard U P, 1965.
2. Rollins, Hyder Edward, ed. *The Keats Circle*. Vol. 1. Cambridge: Harvard U P, 1965.
3. Ward, Aileen. *John Keats: The Making of a Poet*. New York: Farrar, 1968.
4. Severn, Joseph. *Letters and Memoirs*.

5. Ibid.
6. Ibid.

Last Portrait: Of His Hand

1. Rollins, Hyder Edward, ed. *The Keats Circle*. Vol. 2. Cambridge: Harvard U P, 1965.
2. Rollins, Hyder Edward, ed. *The Keats Circle*. Vol. 1. Cambridge: Harvard U P, 1965.
3. Ibid.
4. Ibid.
5. Keats. "This living hand, now warm and capable."

INDEX